Victor's War

The World War II Letters of Lt. Col. Victor Delnore

Edited by

Patricia Delnore Magee

TURNER PUBLISHING COMPANY

Paducah, Kentucky

TURNER PUBLISHING COMPANY
412 Broadway • P.O. Box 3101
Paducah, Kentucky 42002-3101
(270) 443-0121

Turner Publishing Company Staff:
Dayna L. Williams, Editor
Shelley R. Davidson, Designer

Library of Congress Control No: 00-106212
ISBN 978-1-63026-948-7

Additional copies may be purchased directly
from the publisher.
Limited Edition.

DEDICATION

This book is dedicated to my father,
who wrote the letters,
and to my mother, who inspired them.

ACKNOWLEDGEMENTS

I am grateful to several people for their help in the various stages of writing this book. At the University of Delaware, Professor Marcia Peoples Halio and Reference Librarian Linda Stein gave me practical advice that got the project off to a solid start. My husband, Professor James Magee, taught me how to use a computer and unsnagged more technical problems than I care to remember. His patience and constant support were a tremendous boon.

Fred Brown and Bill Dupuis, of the Boylston Historical Society, offered advice about the publishing business, as well as tremendous support throughout the project. Judith Haynes, corresponding secretary of BHS, undertook the laborious task of proofreading an early draft of the manuscript.

Turner editor Dayna Williams deserves special recognition. Her diligence, creativity and attentiveness to every detail made preparing the book for publication a joyful experience for me.

My father's brother, Charles Abdelnour, and cousins, Albert and Adele Abdelnour, helped to clarify facts related to the early history of my father's family, as well as the sad details of my Uncle Underwood Abdelnour's death in a German POW camp in northern France.

My brother, Victor, Jr., graciously lent me several photographs from his baby album, as well as newspaper clippings and other memorabilia that came into his possession after our father's death. He and my sister Cathy were a constant source of encouragement as this project evolved from a typewriting task into a book.

Finally, I want to express special thanks to my mother, Catherine Delnore, who patiently answered my questions about details contained in the letters, offered me tremendous support throughout the project, and generously allowed me to open her private world to public view.

Patricia Delnore Magee
Newark, Delaware
January 2001

CONTENTS

INTRODUCTION

On May 24, 1998, my father, Victor Delnore, died in a nursing home in West Boylston, Massachusetts, a few miles from my parents' Boylston home and not far from the Worcester neighborhood where he grew up. A few days later, he was buried in nearby Paxton. The proximity of these four locations suggests a life whose geographical span was very narrow. Nothing could be further from the truth.

In the course of his 84-year life, my father worked in, resided in, traveled in, and fought in dozens of countries around the world. In fact, stating that Worcester was his hometown is somewhat misleading because this overlooks the fact that he spent the first two years of his life in the British West Indies. His parents, Melhem and Nozly Abdelnour, were Lebanese immigrants, heading west to seek a better life, which for them meant any life that was different from the one that they had been living in Lebanon. Their poverty and alien status forced them to travel by whatever affordable transportation was available. They followed a very circuitous route from Lebanon to England (where fortunately they were unsuccessful in their attempt to buy tickets for the sold-out transatlantic maiden voyage of the Titanic) to the West Indies, and then finally to Boston, where they arrived in 1916. At that time Worcester, Massachusetts was one of the biggest industrial cities in New England, and since factory jobs were one of the few "career opportunities" available to immigrants, the Abdelnour family settled in Worcester.

As the fourth of six children in an immigrant family that could barely support itself, Victor Abdelnour was no stranger to hunger, cold, discrimination, and dead-end jobs. Educational opportunities were almost nonexistent for people like him, with little money and no connections. But Victor was ambitious enough and smart enough to realize that if he wanted to succeed in life, he would have to create his own opportunities. In 1935, he celebrated his 21st birthday as a newly commissioned Second Lieutenant in the U.S. Army. Two years later, he Americanized his name to the easier-to-spell and harder-to-trace Delnore.

Ambition and intelligence served him well. In early 1940, he persuaded 20-year old Catherine Abdelmaseh, also the child of Lebanese immigrants, to marry him. Her parents opposed the union of their daughter to a Catholic, and the fact that she had an older unmarried sister did not help his cause. The couple decided to elope, and they married secretly in Ft. Benning, Georgia, in the fall of 1940. By the time the dust had settled, Catherine's parents decided that all was forgiven and welcomed their new son-in-law with open, albeit Syrian Orthodox, arms. By 1942, Victor was a captain, and a year later, now the proud father of a baby son, he was promoted to major. By early 1945, when he was sent to Europe as commander of the 13th Armored Division's 46th Tank Battalion, he was Lt. Colonel Victor Delnore.

My father's tour of duty in Europe, during the final months and immediate aftermath of World War II, lasted from mid-January to mid-July of 1945. He spent the first several weeks in Normandy, preparing himself and his battalion for combat. In mid-March, the 46th Tank Battalion was assigned to Patton's U.S. Third Army, which spearheaded the final Allied drive through the Ruhr Valley, the industrialized center of Germany. Storming through Germany so fast that they sometimes did not know where they were, they occupied one town after another, taking German prisoners and liberating Allied POWs.

During this hectic period, on April 15, my father was wounded in a particularly gruesome battle, in which he earned not only the Purple Heart, but also the Bronze Star. Just a few days later, he led eleven men on a daring reconnaissance mission to seize the town of Mudlinghoven, the last operational German headquarters in the Ruhr. Two German generals, their staff, and 600 soldiers were captured without a single American casualty, an act for which Lt. Col. Delnore was awarded the Silver Star.

Reaching the Austrian border by the end of April, the 46th Tank Battalion crossed the Inn River and occupied the town of Braunau, birthplace of Adolf Hitler. Here they liberated a camp of 15,000 Allied prisoners, 4,200 of them Americans. By this point, three key countries in the World War had lost their leaders. In rapid succession, Franklin Delano Roosevelt died of a stroke on April 12, the deposed Benito Mussolini was assassinated on April 28, and Adolf Hitler committed suicide on April 30. Germany was only days away from surrender, which was officially proclaimed on May 8, 1945.

From early May until the end of June, the job of the 46th Tank Battalion was essentially to serve as a military police force in the Braunau area. In the last phase of its European tour of duty, the battalion returned to France and prepared for the journey home, eventually departing from Le Havre on July 14th, the French Day of Independence.

During his 6-month separation from his wife and baby son, my father wrote to my mother nearly every day. She saved his letters, most of them V-mails (for easier handling by the Post Office, the original letters were photocopied, shrunk to postcard size, and patriotically christened "V-mails"), along with a few photographs he had sent. Unfortunately, as a combat soldier who had to keep his baggage at an absolute minimum, my father could not hold on to my mother's letters. When he returned home in late July of 1945, he assembled his half of the correspondence into a little folder and stashed it away in an Army trunk. In the years that followed, the trunk moved with the Delnore family from one Army assignment to the next — an area that spanned three continents — and finally came to a stop in the basement of the Boylston, Massachusetts home where my parents settled in 1976. The trunk remained unopened, the letters lay undisturbed and forgotten, for 53 years.

In the months following his death in 1998, as my mother was performing the arduous task of sorting through my father's clothes, papers, and other belongings, she discovered the letters, still neatly assembled as my father had left them. For her the idea of rereading them was too painful to contemplate so soon after his death, and so she willingly passed them on to me. With my mother's encouragement, I began the task of typing the letters into a more legible manuscript. This was no simple project. Their sheer number, my father's very small handwriting, and the fact that most of the letters were V-mails — all resulted in a transcription job that required long hours, patience, and, frequently, a magnifying glass.

At the outset, the goal was to produce a document that family members could read to learn about my father's wartime experiences. My brother, sister, and I knew next to nothing about the subject, since my father practically never spoke about it, and then only in the vaguest of terms. Once when the family was driving through Germany in the 1950's, my father stopped the car on a country road, pointed to an open field near a river, and told us that this was the place where, nine years earlier, he had been wounded in combat. Later, in 1960, on the day he left our home in California to begin a year-long tour of duty in Saudi Arabia, my mother found tucked under her pillow the old Army sweater that he had been wearing when he was shot. That sweater, somewhat tattered and with the bullet hole in the shoulder patched with darning thread, had great sentimental value to him, and he left it as a parting token of his love.

Apart from these two incidents, the only war stories that my father ever told related to his job of liberating Allied prisoners as the 46th Tank Battalion rolled through Germany, and even this he talked about, to me at least, only once. We three children had the strong impression that my father considered his participation in World War II a necessary, but terrible, experience. He had no desire to dwell on those memories or to put a "guts and glory" spin on his life as a combat soldier.

Victor, Catherine, and Victor, Jr., in a family portrait taken in Brownwood, Texas, in December 1944, shortly before my father's departure

Although the project began as an attempt simply to learn about my father's wartime experiences and to share this knowledge with my family, it soon became evident that the letters had historical and literary merit. It was also clear that since they contained so many references to unfamiliar people and long past events, some serious editing would be necessary. Fellow soldiers, family members, neighborhood happenings, news from the battlefront, military slang, childhood reminiscences — all had to be identified, defined, or elaborated on. Before long the project began to take on a life of its own, as I interviewed relatives, consulted World War II history books,

Victor and Catherine Delnore, Ft. Benning, Georgia, 1940

pored over my father's copies of *History of the 13th Armored Division* and *13th Armored Division*, and scanned the television guide each week so as not to miss any World War II documentaries.

I also had to deal with the fact that at times my father revealed an unsympathetic side. He could be impatient, dogmatic, and patronizing toward my mother, and these flaws are evident in some of his letters. My father also had great integrity, and, out of respect for his honesty, I chose not to alter the unflattering passages.

I hope that this correspondence makes compelling and informative reading for anyone who is interested in one of the most significant eras in modern history. The fact that most of the young men and women who lived through World War II have now, like my father, passed away, makes the preservation of their memory even more important. However, beyond their historical value, the letters are important for another story that they tell, the story of a man who, though separated from his family by 3,000 miles, and though a combat soldier in a deadly war, steadfastly remained a husband, father, brother, and son.

Major Delnore, 1943

CHAPTER *I*

THE VOYAGE TO EUROPE

"TAKING THE VOYAGE LIKE A GOOD SAILOR."

The first group of letters, dated from January 16-29, was written aboard the military ship that carried my father from New York to France. Most of them, indeed most of the entire correspondence, are V-mails. Because of strict military censorship, my father was not permitted to name the ship (the SS *Sea Quail*) nor the French port of destination (bomb-shattered Le Havre). The overall tone of these early letters is romantic and nostalgic. My father recalled the "second honeymoon" that he and my mother enjoyed in the Brooklyn home of a relative before his departure for Europe. He inquired and reminisced about his 18-month old son, Victor, Jr., and he mentioned a few domestic concerns, such as working out a financial agreement to pay his mother-in-law for his wife and son's room and board in her home in Worcester. The most serious problem that he discussed in any detail was his effort to resist seasickness, an ailment that appears to have afflicted almost everyone aboard ship. Clearly his intention was to reassure his wife (and himself!) that he was faring well.

While the mood is mostly lighthearted, my father also revealed some serious and practical concerns. Having been born in Jamaica, West Indies of Lebanese parents who later immigrated to the United States, he had become a U.S. citizen when he was nearly 18. A few of the letters allude to his efforts to obtain official papers from the Military Intelligence Division to confirm his American citizenship. Another concern was the transfer of household goods to Massachusetts from Texas, where he and others from the 13th Armored Division had trained for combat. Victor Delnore was not a man who left problems unresolved, and his early letters revealed a desire to remain involved in domestic and business matters, even though he was a soldier on his way to war.

A very somber subject that must have weighed heavily on his mind surfaced in his January 17 letter, in which he asked my mother to let him know if his parents were "still taking the news about Undy badly." Undy was the nickname of my father's older brother Underwood Abdelnour, a Captain in the Air Corps, who was assigned to the U.S. Intelligence Division during World War II. In August of 1944, Capt. Abdelnour and two others, 1st Lieutenants Blanton Haskell and Frank Symington, were on a mission in northern France. The men thought that they were traveling through territory recently captured by the Allies; in fact, it had been reoccupied by the Germans. Their jeep was ambushed and fired upon, and Lt. Symington, the driver, was shot in the abdomen and lost control of the jeep. At the time, the War Department was unable to determine their fate, and for about one year the men were classified as "missing in action."

After the war ended, the Abdelnour family was notified of Underwood's death, but the details of the circumstances surrounding his capture and death remained a mystery until later. Family members interviewed in early 2000 recalled that in 1946 or 1947, they received a phone call from Blanton Haskell, who subsequently visited them to relate what he knew of the failed mission. According to Haskell, Lt. Symington had died from his abdominal wound soon after his capture. Underwood had been shot in the thigh and was taken to a prison hospital to be treated. Haskell was placed in a nearby POW camp. When Haskell inquired about his comrade a few days after their capture, his German guards informed him that Underwood was dead. They reported that, although his leg wound was not serious, the German medics had not realized until too late that Underwood was bleeding internally from a ruptured spleen.

In January 1945, my father knew only that his brother was missing in action. In subsequent letters written shortly before his return from Europe, he described his attempts to get to Brest "to check up on Undy," who, he hoped and trusted, was still alive.

16 January 45
No. 1

Dearest Catherine,

I can't begin to tell you how much I enjoyed the last weekend with you. I'll always treasure it as a sort of second honeymoon. Outside of your usual habit of going to sleep on me during shows, everything was really fine.

Your Uncle Asa and his family were really nice to us. Couldn't have been nicer.

I am mailing my shortcoat home to you. If it fits Charlie*, let him have it.

I hope my little Daddee ** wasn't too much trouble for the folks. They would never admit it if he were. Tell him I love him and his Mommy very much.

Daddy (Big)

*Charles Abdelnour, my father's younger brother. The names of people who could be identi-
fied are cited in footnotes at the bottom of the letter in which they first appear. A few
names, such as Uncle Asa, are identifiable from the context.

**one of my father's nicknames for baby son, Victor, Jr. Other nicknames, mentioned in
subsequent letters, were "my shadow" and "Ah-Goo."

17 January 45

Dearest Catherine,

I have written the Military Intelligence Division at Washington and asked them to send you the Certificate of Derivative Citizenship, which is sup-posed to have been issued to me. Enclosed you will find a copy of the letter I sent. Please file this for me for future reference. If you have not received the certificate in about two weeks, please write and ask for it.

Honey, I hope you have started writing to me because I'm going to be lonesome for your letters. Please start writing now rather than wait for let-ters from me, as my mail will be slow in getting to you.

Has Victor started to miss me yet? I sure hope not. Get someone to toss him around as I did and I think he'll be ok. Catherine, you ought to buy him a chap stick to rub on his lips to prevent chapping.

I sent you a little gift yesterday which I couldn't resist buying you. I wrote you a little message on the cover of the box.

Please be considerate of my folks and please let me know if they are still taking the news about Undy badly.

I love you.
Vic (Big)

18 January 45
Letter #3, Somewhere on the High Seas

My Dearest Catherine,

At last we are parted, but for a short time I hope. I have received all your letters to include the one you wrote me from Brooklyn. That is as nice a letter as any I have ever received from you. I shall treasure it always. I have already read it about five times.

I like the way you refer to our little boy. He sure is a character. My thoughts so far since our parting have been constantly of you and him. One of the cute things he has done cannot be erased from my mind. I have reference to the night during our last week in Brownwood* when he left his crib and started to join the little radio-listening session we were having in our room. Remember how he opened the door and peered out. The little son-of-a-gun knew he had no business leaving his bed, but he sure was going to try it. Remember how he tried to smile me out of it when I ordered him back to bed, and how shocked and angry he acted when I insisted. The little beggar did go back to bed then, didn't he?

---

*In 1944, my parents lived in Brownwood, Texas. My father was stationed at Camp Bowie, where part of the 13th Armored Division trained in preparation for combat duty in Europe.

They say children don't understand anything while they are really young. You and I know that to be wrong, else why did he go back to bed against his desires? He knew he'd get a whoppin'.

Don't have much news for you as yet. Nothing unusual or exciting has happened since our parting. I hope you have made a financial agreement with your mother by now. Please let me know when you purchase the bonds and when you receive the certificate on citizenship from Washington. Also, write the Registrar of Births at Kingston, Jamaica, BWI and ask for my birth certificate.

Love,
Vic (Big)

25 January 45
Letter #4, Still on the High Seas

Dearest Catherine,

So far we have been having an uneventful trip. Nothing unusual has happened. Weather at first was really fine, but for two days we have experienced some really rough weather. So far I haven't been sick, bit dizzy at times though. Feldman* has been sick throughout the voyage. Hasn't eaten a meal. Sheffey ** is in good shape. I'm a better sailor than I thought I would be. Col. Holt is tops. Best sailor on board.

Catherine, when you write use "v-mail", much quicker.

I hope that by now you have adjusted yourself and are getting along ok. Please write me often and tell me about my shadow.

Vic (Big)

*Maj. Eugene M. Feldman, on the staff of the 46th Tank Battalion
**Maj. John P. Sheffey, also on the staff of the 46th Tank Battalion

29 January 45
#5

Dearest Catherine,

Still taking the voyage like a good sailor — didn't know I was that good. Kitty, I do hope that you have received all our freight from Brownwood in good shape. Please let me know.

I would like very much to have a picture of you and Victor. I've seen some in pretty folders about 5 x4 . Really nice. Send the old man one. You on one side, the Daddee on the other. Make it really good. Don't rush things and get any old thing.

Love,
Vic (Big)

Chapter II

First Six Weeks in France: Preparing for Combat

"Life to date has been extremely pleasant."

The sequence of this next group of letters starts out a bit confusing. In a letter dated January 28, my father described getting settled in France, although the previous letter, dated January 29, was apparently written while he was still at sea. The 50th Anniversary edition of the *History of the 13th Armored Division* reports that the 46th Tank Battalion debarked in Le Havre in the dead of night on January 31, 1945. Since later letters reveal that all of these early ones were written under heavy censorship regulations, it is probable that my father fabricated certain events, dates, and locations, and may have gotten his facts confused during those hectic first days in France.

Throughout February and until mid-March of 1945, the 46th Tank Battalion was billeted in a small Norman village northwest of Paris. As battalion commander, my father and his staff were quartered in a beautiful château about 150 yards from the battalion headquarters. Censorship regulations prevented him from naming the location, but did not prevent him from describing in great detail the château and its resident family, the Wermaires. In fact, in his letter dated February 8, he enclosed three picture postcards of the château. On the photo of the front facade, he labeled the various parts of the mansion, teasingly pointing out that the blond and beautiful Nicole, daughter-in-law of Monsieur and Madame Wermaire, had a room right next to his.

Here and elsewhere, my father did not hesitate to show his flirtatious side. Coy observations about Nicole's underwear and chatty visits from and to Red Cross women created a certain unmistakable effect. Perhaps he was trying to arouse jealousy in my mother. A more important side of himself, expressed much more often, was that of a loving husband and devoted father. He wrote to my mother that he spent most of his spare time "just thinking of what you and my shadow are doing at any particular moment." Separated from the family he cherished, he assured my mother that "you are becoming dearer and dearer to me with each passing day." He also wrote two letters on March 7, one of them addressed directly to "My Dear Little Daddee."

During those winter weeks in Normandy, when my father was in good spirits, he wrote of his admiration for the brave French people, his satisfaction with the good food and comfortable accommodations, his enjoyment of informal social events involving the American Red Cross women housed nearby, and his delight in the pleasant weather and smooth mail delivery system. When he was in a less pleasant frame of mind, he commented on the unattractive appearance of the French women, expressed exasperation with my mother for failing to send him photos of her and the baby, complained about the cold and the rain, and criticized the erratic mail delivery system. Understandably, his moods influenced his perceptions and attitudes.

While stationed in northern France, my father routinely visited Belgium for several days at a time. What he misleadingly referred to as "sightseeing trips" were, in fact, important educational experiences in which he "learned plenty from his fellow officers." Military censorship prevented him from elaborating, but surely those trips were an important part of his preparation for leading the 46th Tank Battalion into combat.

At least one trip that my father made during this period was for pure pleasure. His March 4 letter mentioned his long-awaited visit to Paris, which had been liberated by the Allies in August of 1944. On March 6, in one of the liveliest and most vivid letters in the entire correspondence, he wrote a detailed account of his Paris experience. Clearly he delighted in the cafes, the dance halls, and the company of the French women. Reading his account of how he apologized for his "extremely ugly" appearance in his battlefield uniform, only to be told by his companions that in the eyes of the grateful French people the American soldier was the best dressed man in town, one can easily sense his pride and delight.

28 January 45
#6, Somewhere in France

Dearest Catherine,

It sure feels good to have my feet on dry land again. The part of France I am in looks just like New England. Hills and tall trees. Right now the weather is miserable. Snow, rain, sleet, and cold for about a week. Visited Le Havre yesterday.

We are quartered in a French château, which defies description, it's so big and beautiful. I'll just have to send you a picture of it. By "we" I mean only me and my staff: Sheffey, Deters*, Feldman, Etchells**, and Willerton***. The family still lives in it and are extremely nice. There are at least 25 rooms in the house. Two of them are each as big as the Knights of St. George's Hall****. My room is as big as parlor and dining room together in your mom's house.

Love,
Vic (Big)

*1 Lt. Fred H. Deters, Adjutant on the Staff of the 46th Tank Battalion
**Capt. John C. Etchells, Commander, Company A of the 46th Tank Battalion
***Capt. Arthur M. Willerton, S-2 on the Staff of the 46th Tank Battalion
****The Social Hall in St. George's Syrian Orthodox church in Worcester, Massachusetts

2 February 45
#7

Hello Sweetheart,

Things are a bit slow right now, so I thought I would drop you a line. I received four letters from you yesterday. The last was postmarked 9:00 PM on the 19th. Glad to see you liked the little gift I sent you. I thought you would.

The French people sure are nice to me. Anything we want we can have. Kids follow our soldiers everywhere.

Got a look at the city of Rouen yesterday. Sure is beautiful though somewhat damaged.

Haven't made any use of the Sweetheart soap as yet. Haven't had time, nor have I seen anyone I'd be interested in. The old man always was fussy, you know.

Please write more about my little man in your letters.

Love,
Vic (Big)

7 February 45
#7

Dearest Catherine,

Just received a "V" mail letter from you in which you ask me to write more than once a week. Okay, it's a deal if you write every day. Sweetheart, date your letters. It's one old American custom you were taught at school.

Sorry to hear the little fellow is beginning to act spoiled — too many grandparents, uncles, and whatnot. I believe ignoring him is better than punishing him.

Have you received our stuff from Brownwood yet?

Where the heck is the picture you promised me?

Love,
Vic (Big)

8 February 45
#8

Dearest Catherine,

Nothing new — just another letter. Weather here is breaking. Natives say it is the first sign of spring. Fine. Could be warmer.

Am sending you a picture of the château where I live. Words will never describe it. The fellows and I are really comfortable.

Honey, please rush that picture I asked you for. I really need it and want it.

You haven't said anything in your mail about buying the War Bonds. Please let me know. Also if you are getting the monthly allotment and War Bond. Should have started coming now.

Vic (Big)

8 February 45
#9

Hello Darling,

Weather here is atrocious although there are some signs of it clearing. Thank God it has not been cold. This business of writing you every day makes it kind of hard on the old man as I run out of things to say.

The food has been A-1 so far. The rations put out to overseas troops are something to behold. I feel a bit embarrassed eating it when I see how badly off the French people are.

People here have not been able to buy new clothes for 4 1/2 years, and it is a bit rough on their appearance. Some of the girls have silk stockings though, and that is really something.

How is my little shadow making out?

Love,
Vic (Big)

8 February 45

Hello Sweetheart,

Bit late to say so but you still are and always will be my Valentine.

Thought I'd write you an extra special letter because you are my extra special girl. Then, too, prompt as "V" mail is, what can you say in one page?

Here is the dope to date.

Been in France quite a while now and have only had time off to visit two cities — Le Havre and Rouen. While in England was able to visit Portsmouth and Southhampton for a brief time.

As I have previously written you, I am quite comfortable in my present lodgings. I'll try to give you a picture of the place I live as well as the people I am in contact with.

The Château: (I am not permitted to name it as you may be able to locate it geographically and the United States would lose the war because you would know the location of my outfit.) Enclosed you will find two views of it. It speaks for itself. The grounds the château is on is an area about as big as Green Hill Park*, only it is much more heavily treed and far better kept up. It is the prettiest spot I have ever seen in this world. The grounds have two steeplechase courses laid out on them. Two horses are available to anyone who would care to ride. On the grounds we have several beautiful buildings. The buildings are of red brick and are quite large. They are used mainly as homes for the maids, caretaker, and other workers on the estate. In addition, there are several large barns as well as small buildings, placed at random throughout the estate and serving as teahouses, etc. There are two tennis courts on the grounds also. I haven't had time to really look around, but there are other features which I have missed. My Battalion Headquarters building is about 200 yards from the château. It is a two storied brick house and has about 10 rooms.

The owner of all this property is a M. Wermaire. He is about 70 years old, but is as well preserved as our good friend Mr. Tooma. Living with him in the château are his wife, a tall, dignified, beautiful woman of 65 (looks around 45, and a daughter-in-law, Nicole. Nicole is the widow of their eldest

---

*A public park in Worcester, Massachusetts

son, who has since remarried but continues to live with her former in-laws. Her husband works in Paris, where she goes to stay with him periodically. She has a daughter 15 months old, who is as good a baby as our little man. Nicole is about 28 years old, a blond, and beautiful. She, as well as the rest of the family, is extremely well traveled, having visited just about every spot in Europe as well as having been to the good old U.S. They all speak English as well as we do. In addition, they speak Italian, German, and RUSSIAN. About the best way to describe them is that they are just about the Hollywood version of the continental smart set, with the exception that they are not the least bit snooty.

There are several servants living in the château. How many I do not know. Every day I see another one. They have a lower wing in the château and keep to themselves. They really scatter when we come in. Guess the German officers who had been quartered here did a little pinching. In addition to the household servants, there are all kinds of people working and living on the grounds.

The outfit is billeted in the villages surrounding the château. These villages are extremely small — a cluster of 10 houses or a couple of good sized farms go into the making of each of them. Each company is billeted in a village. The company commander and his officers live with the mayor, and the troops live in the barns or villagers' homes. Each village, no matter how small, has a mayor.

The people here really like our troops. They have had the Germans living with them for four years, and they really hate their guts. The Heinies were really rough on them, took their belongings, crowded them off roads, wouldn't let them have church services, etc. In contrast, the Americans ask for things, take only what the people can spare, pay for it, and slow down with vehicles to 5 mph when passing French civilians. Honestly, it just makes me fighting mad to see how the women, through habit, dash for the sides of the roads when they hear a vehicle coming.

The kids are all cute and follow our troops everywhere. They are very small for their age. All look about three years younger than they really are. They are well mannered, never speak unless spoken to except to say hello. They gather around our chow lines, but will ask for nothing to eat, although one look at their eyes will tell you what they are after. If offered anything to eat, they never refuse. Eat anything and as much as you will give them.

With the exception of the Wermaire family, people are extremely poorly dressed. They have been unable to buy clothes for over four years. The rags they wear would be in about the hobo class back home. This places the girls at one hell of a disadvantage and most of the men won't even look at them. Nicole is the only girl in France (outside of the Americans) that I have seen who owns a pair of brassieres and a girdle. Don't ask me how I found out, Mommy! However, with all the shortage on clothes people manage to keep one fairly good change of clothes for church Sunday. People are really hard up. With all that, they are the most cheerful bunch you ever saw.

Life to date has been extremely pleasant. What with being Battalion Commander and the added prestige of being M. Wermaire's guest, I have to be on really good behavior. Most of the French are amazed at my age*. Lieutenant Colonels in the French Army are a good deal older.

That's all for now, Mommy. Please write me every day. I previously told you to write "V" mail, but that's too short, so write regular mail unless you are in a hurry with some dope.

Please send snapshots of yourself and my shadow. I have enclosed three picture postcards of the château.

The Daddy Loves You.

Vic (Big)

P.S. Before sealing the letter, two Red Cross girls stopped in with a donut truck. Took them over to the château to freshen up and to have cocktails. They were very much impressed and wanted to know how come the 46th rated such accommodations. Answer: God always takes care of us. It was a lot of fun to talk to a couple of American girls. These two were a lot of fun and I sure had a great time kidding them. O'Malley** was different as usual. Instead of the girls entertaining him, he had them take it easy while he had his men put on a floorshow for them. Great fun. Nicole was awfully jealous 'cause everyone dropped her like a hot potato to talk to our own girls.

When I started to write this letter, the weather was tops, but now it is getting ready to rain again.

---

*My father was 30 years old.

**Capt. Richard J. O'Malley, Commander of 46th Tank Battalion's Company D

Please, sweetheart, do not worry if you do not get my mail regularly. I will write you every day, no fooling. I am very lonesome for news of my shadow, so start the dope and the pictures flowing.

I love you.
Vic (Big)

My father's early descriptions of the château in Beaunay omitted its exact location. Postcards he mailed home at that time pictured the château, but contained no descriptive details. However, once censorship was lifted (in the summer of 1945), he sent my mother two picture postcards of the château, with detailed descriptions on the back of each, as well as arrows marking the main rooms and other details. He probably mailed these cards home sometime in the late spring of 1945, from Braunau, Austria.

Postcard #1:a view of the front facade of the château, with hills and trees in the background. Various windows are labeled "my room," "Nicole's," "Vermaires' wing," "dining room," and "living room." On the left is arrow marked "B'n Hqs 50 yds." The back of the postcard reads: "At last censorship is off, so I can tell you where we were for our first 6 weeks in France. The château is in the village of BEAUNAY. It's so small you won't find it on the map. It is located about 3 miles southwest of the village of BACQUEVILLE, which in turn is about 10 miles south of DIEPPE, which you should be able to find on most maps. Sheffey and I shared the room shown. Feldman and Wallaston were across the hall from us with the General (French) opposite Nicole. Deters, Etchells, Sam Miller in attic."

Postcard #2: a view of the rear facade of the château. The back of the postcard reads: "cont'd. The living room and dining room together took the whole first floor of the house. The towers were bathrooms upstairs and the coziest little reading and writing rooms downstairs you ever saw. The house had another floor underground. In the old days a moat surrounded the whole thing. There are several other buildings on the estate, in which the help live. All really nice homes. Honestly, you have no idea how wonderful the people in Beaunay and the surrounding villages were to us. Our quarters were better than the [French] General's."

Postcard #3: Another view of the château at Beaunay

10 February 45
#10

Hello Sweetheart,

So far your mail has been terrible. Received four letters in one batch on the 29th and one "V" mail on the 7th. Nothing else. The home front is sure letting us down.

Temperature has taken a terrific drop and it sure is getting into my bones.

Now that Rachel is home, what rearrangements have been made on rooms? Does my little shadow still sleep with his mommy or is he being exclusive? Give with the news, honey.

I still don't know what took Rachel to Buffalo and what brought her back. Or, is it none of my business*?

What is happening to the boys from the hill?**

Give!

The Boss
P.S. Love (afterthought)

*My mother's youngest sister, Rachel Abdelmaseh, had recently moved back to her parents' home in Worcester, after having spent a few cold and homesick months in Buffalo, NY, where she had been working. My grandparents' flat was very small, and so my father was naturally curious to know what living arrangements had been settled on once Rachel returned home.

** My father's boyhood neighborhood in Worcester.

10 February 45
#10

Hello Sweetheart,

Hurray! The sun is shining, although we had one hell of a thunderstorm last night.

Still not doing too much work, but time does not drag 'cause everything here is so new.

Haven't seen a girl yet I'd give a bar of sweetheart soap to. Who knows, they may look better as time goes along. If what I've seen so far is any cross section of the French girls, then the American girls have nothing to fear. Anyway, you don't.

Still have not received any mail except that which I have previously mentioned.

Chow has been better than what we get in the States.

Love,
Vic (Big)

12 February 45
#12

Hello Sweetheart,

Sunday and it's raining again. Never saw a country where it rained so much. Mud all over the place. It has its compensation, however, for it certainly keeps the grass green. Rain is not the Louisiana type, but fine and drizzly like we have at home.

Spent last night exactly as I have spent every other night since I got here. Chatted and played cards over some coffee at the château. Nightlife is absolutely zero. Beginning to get some of the boys down, as we haven't been able to arrange for any movies or entertainment of any type as yet.

On my way to church now. How is my shadow making out? Where the heck are those pictures?

Love,
Vic (Big)

13 February 45
#13

Dearest Sweetheart,

Tuesday and once again the skies are clear. I'll give ten to one that it rains before the day is over.

My daily routine has not changed one bit. Spent last night with the family. They had just returned from Paris and brought along a retired French Major General as their guest. He was most interesting.

Honest, things are really dull here. I spent considerable of my spare time just thinking of what you and my shadow are doing at that particular moment. Bit difficult because of the five hours difference in time. No mail from you as yet.

Love,
Vic (Big)

14 February 45
#14

Hello Darling,

Valentine's Day. Good thing I sent you your present long ago.

I won my bet on the weather yesterday. It started to pour at 1400 and I got caught in the storm. However, the sun is out today, but I'll still give ten to one it rains by suppertime.

Received a "V" mailed letter from you yesterday dated 29 January. Better write me every day or I'll cut your allotment off.

Had a hard time getting time to write this letter in the morning, as is my custom.

I am really hungry for news of you and my little man. I am saving all your letters and reread them constantly. It was just a month ago today that I saw you off on the train.

Love,
Vic (Big)

15 February 45
#15

Dearest Mommy,

Beautiful spring day today. Been reading about the blizzard you've had recently. How does my little man like it? Hope you are not snowbound. Pardonez-moi*.

Had Wogan** over for a desk lunch to meet our French general. Was it ritzy. Worcester was never like this.

Going out on a five-mile hike daily now. Just thought I'd drop you a line cause I love you so much and think of you and the other third of the family constantly.

Mail from you is really poor. Gets me down sometimes, so please write more often. "V" mail is not turning out so good. Mix up the type mail. Regular and "V" and I'll let you know which comes thru faster.

V. (B)

*My father originally omitted the "not," which he inserted later between "are" and "snow-bound." This explains the French apology.

**Maj. Gen. John B. Wogan, commander of the 13th Armored Division

15 February 45
#15A

Hello Sweetheart,

I've already written you one letter today, but since then I have received five letters from you all in one batch. It certainly was enjoyable reading them. Thanks a million, sweetheart, for all the info on the family, you, and my little man. Letters were dated 21 Jan, 25 Jan, 31 Jan, and 1 Feb. One regular long letter undated, but postmarked 20 Jan.

Honey, I think you had better send all your mail regular mail (3 cents). "V" mail has been slow. I enjoy reading the long letters much more. You can send "V" when you are in a hurry. You might try sending both types on the same day and I'll let you know which gets here first.

Love,
Vic (Big)

16 February 45
#16

Hello Sweetheart,

Having a beautiful spring day today. That makes two in a row. Unbelievable around here. Mud has dried off. Pleasure to walk again.

Stayed awake quite a bit last night thinking of you and little Victor. Those five letters all at once were really nice. I can almost see him doing the things you wrote of.

Regarding the citizenship certificate. The letter you received on 18 January was from Boston confirming the telephone call I made. I wrote Washington on about the 16th asking them to send you the certificate. A copy of that letter was sent to you. Let me know when it is answered. If they have not, send them a letter calling their attention to the first and asking them to do something about it.

Furniture should have taken six weeks. You should have it by now.

Love,
Vic (Big)

17 February 45
#17

Hello Sweetheart,

Cloudy this morning. Should be raining by noon. Received a two page "V" mail letter from you yesterday dated 2 Feb. It was a very nice letter. Honey, whatever you did on the insurance is OK. If you ever have any doubts on anything like that, ask Sam*. He has a head on him.

Your letters are wonderful but please make them longer. I like to especially read about incidents pertaining to Ah-Goo and your travels and doings throughout the day. I can close my eyes and actually portray the incidents in my mind.

I'm sorry to hear you miss me so much. You know from past partings how I feel. There is but one solution and that is to keep busy. You might take up your shorthand and typing again, help out Sam, etc. I love you and my shadow very much and think of you constantly.

Vic (Big)

*Sam Abdelmaseh, one of my mother's older brothers

18 February 45
#18

Hello Darling

Received your wonderful valentine today. It sure picked me up. I'm glad I sent you yours from New York, although it was a bit early.

Better not use airmail anymore 'cause your airmail letters take much longer than even regular mail.

It's still pretty early Sunday morning, and as I write this you and the rest of my little family are or should be dead asleep. I intend going to Mass a bit later.

The boys have invited some nurses from a village about 30 miles away to spend the afternoon and to have supper. Unlucky me. Of all days to pick, Gen. Wogan picked today to invite me to supper. Some girl is going to be out of luck.

I still don't know if you purchased the bonds as explained. And I still am waiting for those pictures. Please, honey, send them right away if you haven't already done so. You might send some snapshots of the little man once in a while. I'd like one of him filling my shoes. I'll return them if you want me to. Puh-leeze.

Love,
Vic (Big)

19 February 45
#19

Hello Sweetheart,

Hasn't rained for four days. Record around here. Had a little party for the boys at the château yesterday. Invited over some nurses and Red Cross girls to spend the afternoon and to have supper. Had a very nice time. All the girls insisted on kissing the French general goodnight. He sure enjoyed it.

Honey, the girls over here really have a tough time, but you never hear them complain. They live exactly like the men. Line up for mess, use straddle trenches, etc. They really are wonderful. How they manage to look clean and fresh is beyond me. When I compare what they are doing with what some of the girls we know back home are doing, I get boiling mad.

Enough about that. Tomorrow is my little man's birthday. 19 months old. God bless him and keep him for us. I love you both dearly.

Vic (Big)

20 February 45
#20

Hello Darling,

Ah-Goo is 19 months old today. I spent last evening telling one of the Red Cross girls who had invited me to a movie all about him. I think I talked too much as usual, but I can't help myself when I get on the subject.

Mommy, I'm sure glad that you are doing such a fine job taking care of my shadow. You don't know what a relief it is to know that you are both well, happy, and with our families. Everyone in the division asks me about my strong man. I've caught several of my officers bragging to the French people about what a good egg our little kid is. Even Wogan is a bit guilty. He made the remark at a gathering that if anyone thought this old man was a good dancer, they ought to get a load of his kid on the dance floor.

Things are about the same here. Not working too hard. Meeting more and more of the French people every day. They are really grateful to us for clearing out the Huns, and go to all ends to make us happy. Hope you gave the little man a present from the old man.

Love (lots),
Vic (Big)

February 45
#21

My Dearest Little Sweetheart,

Received your 8 Feb. letter yesterday. Got one from the folks too. I read them over about four times. I have saved all your letters beginning with the one you sent from Memphis while traveling home. By rereading them I get a pretty good idea of how my shadow is getting along.

It certainly was nice of you, Sweetheart, to ask to go to church with my folks. According to their letter you have been really swell, and they think the world of you for being so considerate.

Sweetheart, I hope you have sent the picture I asked for by now. I feel you've let me down on that 'cause I understood you would have the pictures made as soon as you got to Worcester. Here I've received your 8 Feb. letter, which is exactly one month later, and still no picture. What's wrong? Please send the god damned thing.

Honey, I don't need a thing right now. You might start knitting me a couple pair of heavy heavy and I mean heavy wool socks for next winter. It's a real job keeping feet warm in this mud. Oh yeah! Beautiful spring day today. Not a cloud in the sky. Best day we've had. I love you very much.

Vic (Big)

22 February 45
#22

Hello Sweetheart,

Beautiful sunny day today, but a bit on the cold side.

Sweetheart, I appreciate your wanting to send me something, but honestly I need nothing. Brought too much stuff with me. However, I would appreciate it if you would knit me a couple pair of really heavy woolen socks for next winter. Don't rush and send them to me now, as the weather will be warm by the time they get here. Don't make the socks too high — no higher than 11 inches measured from the base of the heel. Any higher and they will come over the top of my combat boots.

Your mail is coming in fairly steady now, and I really enjoy reading it. I hope you've been getting mine steadily. I've numbered them so you could tell if any are missing. I'll start new numbers each month. You might write me longer letters and enclose some snapshots of yourself and the little fellow (If you haven't sent the picture portrait of yourself and Ah-Goo by now, I'm going out with a French girl, so help me.). I particularly like to read about the things the little man has done.

That crack you made in one of your letters about having to be good in order to set a good example for the rest of the boys is no joke, pal. It's the truth. I really do have to, but so help me, it's really easy after looking at the French girls. They really are badly off. No clothes. They all have chapped legs. They look raw. Don't know how they stand it. Course the French aristocrats are better off, but there aren't very many of them.

I spend most of my days working, but not too hard. Evenings play bridge with the family in the château. We've located some American girls lately. There are a couple hundred nurses and Red Cross girls here awaiting assignment. They are housed in a château, which could easily house 1,000. They aren't allowed out evenings unless it is something real special, and then they have to go in groups of five.

The boys have been going over evenings to visit them. There are about 12 chairs in the whole place, no piano, no sign of a radio, no PX, no nothing at all. So you just sit and talk about the good old U.S.A. But even at that it is really enjoyable as they are a bunch of swell kids. Any time we think it's tough on us, we just think of them. Imagine that many girls living together. In their own words, they just feel like screaming at one another. I get along really swell with them, and believe it or not, they call me "Daddy." Here's why. Of all the officers who go there, I've been the only one to openly admit to being married. I spend most of my time telling about you and Ah-Goo. I don't know what's wrong with the fellows 'cause the girls aren't dumb. Their motto is "Treat them all like married men 'cause they in all probability are."

Some of our best friends are having a tough time. Having stated for the first date that they weren't married, they have to keep it up, but the girls aren't really fooled. The ones I'm really sorry for are Sheffey, Feldman, Pfeiffer, and Elmes*. They swear up hill and down that they are single, pull out pay data card, emergency addressee card, etc., to prove it, but the girls just smile tolerantly. We're all married, say they, so married I am, say I, and go on from there to have a fairly good time.

---

*Capt. Kenneth S. Elmes, S-4 on the Staff of the 46th Tank Battalion

Honey, I'm sorry to hear that you miss me as much as you do. I hope you get over it 'cause it is a really tough feeling. I felt the same way for the first three weeks after parting, but have gotten over it now, although I get a recurring spell now and then. I love you and you only, as you well know. I do miss you and my little man very much. This doggoned war will be over some day and we can go back to a normal life once again. Chin up!

Sweetheart, the attached letter is self-explanatory. If you haven't received the certificate, send out a couple of letters — one to White in Washington and one to the San Antonio office. That ought to do it.

If you haven't already sent for my birth certificate, please do so.

I love you very dearly.

Victor (Big)

23 February 45

#23, Somewhere in Belgium

Dearest Sweetheart,

Am on my way up on a sightseeing trip to see Matt Kane* and a few other friends. Nothing at all to get excited about. Very lucky to get the chance.

Your mail is coming in beautifully, and I sure enjoy reading and rereading it. Spent an hour last night rereading all your mail.

Glad to hear that the little fellow is getting along so good in his training. I understand what you meant by the remark "he thinks it's funny." I'm very happy to see that you are enjoying our son so much. That's why I left him with you — to take my place.

I love you very much and think of you constantly. Be back to my château very shortly.

The Daddy (Big)

*Lt. Col. Matthew Kane. In some of the Army history books, his last name is spelled Caine, in others, Kane.

24 February 45
#24, Somewhere in Luxembourg

Dearest Sweetheart,

Passed through several large French cities on the way up. Inasmuch as Thornton* and I were alone, I had a good chance to look around. I was terribly disappointed in the appearance of all the cities. They are old and decrepit. It's not all a result of the war either. It's their age plus the fact that the French just don't seem to give a damn. Carson City, Nev. would be about typical of the French towns I have seen except that the structure is brick instead of wood, and they always manage a beautiful church. Greatly disappointed.

Now Luxembourg, that is something else. Beautiful. That is, what I saw of it, which wasn't too much.

Sweetheart, have you written away for the War Bond or Bonds that are cached away in Washington?

Received the word about Turkey's entry into the war. I'll give $100 for every Turk soldier that gets on the German front. Too late. May help a bit against the Japs though.

Love,
Vic (Big)

*T/5 William H. Thornton, my father's driver

25 February 45
#25

Hello Mommy,

Sunday again. A beautiful day if ever I saw one. Hope the weather holds out.

I'm up here with Hank Davall. He's showing me the ropes and boy is he good. He looks and acts the same. Has developed a habit of knocking on wood every time he makes a statement which has anything to do with not getting hurt.

I hope you and my little man are getting along fine. Your old man is. Have lost hardly any weight. Chow has been too good. Better than back in the States.

Pardon this damned blotting*. It's this lousy French ink.

I love you and my little fellow very very much and think of you constantly.

Vic (Big)

*This letter has four ink smears.

⋙⟩⟨⋘

26 February 45
#26

Hello Sweetheart,

Am still on the sightseeing trip I told you about. Today I'm with Matt Kane. I dropped in at a very busy time; consequently he was not able to give me much time. However, I tagged along. It was very interesting, and I believe I learned plenty. Matt has not changed one bit except that he is much more careful than he used to be during maneuvers.

Ran into Paul Trulord. He commands a company in Matt's outfit. Also ran into several of our old friends from the old days at Polk*. Sgt. Work (wife from Worcester) is now a senior warrant officer, Mule Yarborough and several of my old enlisted men. They were all glad to see me and loaded me down with enough food to last for a week when I asked for a couple of K rations.

I love you very much.

Vic (Big)

*Camp Polk in Louisiana, where my father was stationed in 1941.

27 February 45
#27, Somewhere in Germany

Just got back again with Hank Davall. I intend to spend the next four days with him, after which I'll go back to my outfit.

Got a little break on the last trip and was able to get a bit of time off to visit Liege. What a town. Vive la Belgique. Any crack heretofore made about French girls strictly does not go for the girls of Liège. Had a good time, but it only made me miss the mommy all the more. Belgians speak French, so I got along famously.

On returning, first person I bumped into was Andy Stalker. Still a major. Hasn't changed one bit.

Mommy, since I started this trip, I naturally have not received any mail from you 'cause it would take too long to forward. I'm looking forward to enjoying a huge batch of it when I get back. I only hope you haven't written for any information or anything important. Still have not rec'd word you are receiving my mail.

Love,
Vic (Big)

28 February 45
#28

Hello Mommy,

Still up here with Hank Davall. Things are very interesting. Seeing and learning a lot. I do miss not getting your mail, but look forward to reading a whole batch of it when I get back to my outfit. Have already become the owner of several German weapons, which I intend sending to you as soon as I am allowed to. Weather here has been off and on but not cold.

Living has been fairly comfortable. Haven't slept in a tent or out in the open one night yet. We just move in on a German family, allow them so many rooms, and take the rest to ourselves (beds and all). I am very gratified to see how the Americans are treating German civilians. Never speak or smile to them. If necessary, will order them around. Absolutely no fooling of any kind. Germans don't understand it. Expected something different.

I love you very much.

Vic (Big)

1 March 45
#1

Hello Sweetheart,

Still keeping up my record of writing you a letter a day. Starting a new series of numbers for the new month. I do hope that you are getting my mail ok.

So far this war is more comfortable than maneuvers. Rations are better. In addition, we get a liquor ration each month, that is, the officers do. Got a quart of whiskey, cognac, gin, and champagne. Best quality. Get good radio programs even right up on the shooting front. Newspapers and magazines are adequate. I have lost little of my weight so quit worrying about me getting so slim and handsome that another girl will get me. I don't want anyone but my little gal and my shadow.

Ran into Art Sargent yesterday. He's doing well. Margie has no kids. Is staying in California with her mother. Sweetheart, I love you dearly.

Vic (Big)

2 March 45
#2

Hello Sweetheart,

Bit early in the morning so I don't have much news on the day's activities. Bit cold today, otherwise beautiful. It is now 0830 here; that means 0330 in Worcester and you and my little shadow are pounding the pillow. I spent a good deal of the night thinking of you both, and I could just visualize my little guy standing by the sink, pointing to it and asking for some water. Somehow, usually when I think of him, it is that pose. Although I've never seen him do it, I figure it is about the same as asking for a cookie.

As I've told you before, I've run into a good many of our friends up here. Most of them asked about you and asked me to send you their best. I don't know how you do it but everyone likes you. Poor me, I've got no one but my family to love me. Sweetheart, I love you and my shadow very very much.

Vic (Big)

3 March 45
#3

Hello Sweetheart,

Trip is about over and am ready to start back tomorrow. It has been very interesting. I would not have missed it for the world. I've seen a good many of my old friends. They all seem to be doing well.

I sure have missed not getting your mail, but am looking forward to a whole batch of it at one time. I particularly miss the dope on my Daddee. You know how I love to discuss or read about him.

I hope to be able to visit Paris on my return. Sure would like at least one night in the old town after all I've heard of it. Will let you know how I make out.

People here say the winter has been unusually severe. I think they are nuts. Weather has been relatively warm but rainy (until of late). Not at all bad.

I love you.

Vic (Big)

4 March 45
#4, Back in France

Well Honey,

Your old man finally did get to good old Parree. It certainly is a beautiful place, although a bit dirty now on account of the war. I have never seen women so dressed up in my life. How they do it is beyond me. No fuel for heat, no soap, no new clothes, etc. Yet they all turn out as smart as you please...silk stockings perfume, and all.

They sure think a lot of the Americans. Really nice to us, although there is that usual conscienceless group that profiteer. A ten minute ride in a horse cab cost me 300 francs, the equivalent of $6.00. The Metro (subway) is free to soldiers, but the doggoned thing stops running at 2300, about the time I get started. Will write you a special letter later telling you about my trip.

Love,
Vic (Big)

5 March 45
#5

Hello Sweetheart,

Back with the outfit again. Sure missed my old gang. Have spent the last hour catching up with your mail. Sure makes good reading. Here are the answers to questions you raised.

1. Don't worry about birth certificate. It will come. If it doesn't, so what?
2. Write Transportation Office, Camp Bowie about furniture.
3. I forgive you for not buying bonds on time.
4. Hope you have allotment by now. Pay was 3 wks late.

5. Didn't take any soap to Paris. Supply is intact except for two bars given to Nicole when she left for Paris to stay with her husband.

6. I still love you.

7. I'm right on the citizenship papers. They're in San Antonio. I have written and asked that they be sent to you.

Your mail jumped from 15 Feb to 26 Feb, which is last letter received. Rest are slow. Airmail is waste of money. I think, however, that last letter sure was fast.

Love,

Vic (Big)

6 March 45

My Dearest Catherine,

Received another batch of mail from you after I wrote you yesterday. Had a very enjoyable evening reading it and thinking of you and my little Daddee. From the tone of your, Charlie's, Najla's*, and Rachel's letters, he really must be coming along. I'm very happy that you are enjoying him so much 'cause that is what he is for.

Sweetheart, your mail is coming in beautifully now. I only hope it keeps up. I prefer long letters to "V" mail — much more interesting and just as fast. Along with your letters I received a letter from Rachel, Naj, and two from Chick**. Rachel says she loves my little man very much and is going to wait for him to grow up to marry her. I don't know of a nicer girl so they both have my blessing.

Mommy, you keep asking me if there is anything you can send me. Well, honey, I'd like a 1lb. package of cocoa, a couple jars of mustard, and a few boxes of raisins. Oh yes! A package (small) of salt. Sounds crazy but those are the items that are hard to get. Please send only the quantity I asked for 'cause if you send more I can't carry it around. Now, are you happy?

---

*Najla Abdelnour, my father's younger sister

**nickname of my father's brother Charles

I suppose you would like to know about my trip to Paris. Well, here goes.

Arrived at Paris at 1100 and called up a family that one of the boys had recommended to me. They were very nice and invited me to dinner. I don't know how they did it but they had some beef. We had small steaks, French fries, and a mess of other stuff. Plenty to drink too.

There are four girls in the family. Two daughters, Belita, 25, a knockout, divorced, speaks Russian, French, Italian, and English; Jeannette, 23, even prettier, happily married but hubby away, speaks Russian, French, and English, English with slang expressions, knows all the latest song hits, the nearest thing to an American I've seen this side of the water, always jitterbugging around; a cousin Jeanette, very chic and continental, divorced, also speaks four languages; the last, Germaine, widow, 26, brunette, looks typically French and speaks only French. I forgot, Belita knows a little Arabic, mostly words girls should not know. The four taken together were as nice a group as I have ever seen. Extremely well dressed. As good as anything I have ever seen. Loaded down with jewels and what have you.

Honestly, Mommy, your Daddy (big) did not know what he was getting into. We took off to see the town in one of those French horse buggies you've seen in the movies. Drove around for about two hours looking at all the famous buildings and what have you that Paris if famous for. Very interesting and worthwhile 'cause it certainly is different. Paris, unlike most French cities, has been little touched by war 'cause it was declared an open city. Outside of streets being dirty due to a lack of cleaning facilities, the coldness in the interior of buildings (no heat), lack of food and the shortage of vehicles on the streets, you'd never know a war was going on. The streets just teem with people, extremely crowded over the whole city. People walk just to have something to do and to keep warm plus the fact that they have always liked to parade around just like we do on Easter Sunday.

After driving around we started taking in the cafes. When I saw the prices I almost passed out 'cause I didn't have money enough to last an hour. However, I worried needlessly 'cause, believe it or not, the girls paid for everything. Entertainment for the whole evening came to around $120.00 in our money. However, that would be but around $30.00. The difference exists because the franc, which is valued by the French at approximately 1/2 cent is evaluated by our government, which is seeking to stabilize the value of the franc at 2 cents.

That means that when the government pays me $1.00, they are actually giving me only 25 cents in purchasing value. Bit rough on the American soldiers, but I guess it is absolutely necessary for two reasons, first, as I said, to increase and stabilize the value of the franc; and second, to discourage us from competing with the French in purchasing articles which we don't need but which they do. In any case, they want us to send our dough home where it belongs. I hope that is clear.

I naturally protested the girls paying my way, but they only laughed at me, made me buy them a pretty corsage each, and ended up by calling me a gigolo, but a very handsome one. Honestly, Honey, I don't know how to tell you how I felt. Those kids were dressed like a million dollars and looked and acted like two million, and there I was with about $60.00 in my pocket and my little battlefield uniform, except for my steel helmet, on. You know those high rough, ugly GI shoes with the two ugly buckles (not the ones I had fixed at the shoemaker's), dark pants, that dark GI shirt that I started to throw away more than once, AND WITH MY HELMET LINER, extremely ugly.

When I apologized for my appearance and offered to disappear, you should have seen how nice they were. Told me that they were extremely proud to be with a soldier who had just come from the front, and that in the eyes of the French people I was the best dressed man in town. Sounds like a lot of malarkey, doesn't it? Well, Sweetheart, it wasn't. Honestly, wherever I went I was treated with extreme respect and given priority on seats, etc. over higher ranking officers in blouses and pinks. Wouldn't have believed it possible.

After doing the rounds at the cafes, the girls held a private lottery to see which girl would go dancing with me. Only one could go as girls had to have an escort. Jeanette, the divorced cousin, won (lost?). We went to the Club 45, which is a French Officers Club. The girls had a standing invite. Well, as usual, a few steps on the dance floor and I had Jeanette popeyed. She didn't think that an American could dance as well as your Daddy (big). She really was so dumbfounded that she insisted we go back and get the other girls to come back for a dance each. They dance here same style as the Daddy (big). Long, gliding steps, no bouncing around and no movement from above the waist. Remember what the Daddy (big) has always told you. Well, Pal, all those girls were really good dancers, and you know what the Daddy (big) calls good on the dance floor.

Party broke up at two. Took Jeanette home where the other girls had fixed up a snack and were waiting for us. Finally left after one of the best times (without the Mommy) I have ever had. I liked all four of those kids 'cause they let me talk about my Mommy and my Daddee (little). I showed them pictures, etc. (what little I have — got some more today). They all commented on the different attitude that Americans had for their wives as compared to the French. They are all going to come to America, poison you, and marry me.

Well, Mommy, after all this I am now back with my nose to the grindstone. Have not seen many of the boys at this writing, but those I have seen look good and ask to be remembered to you. They all love you 'cause you make me so happy, thereby making my disposition wonderful and allowing them to get away with murder.

The things I saw on my trip will be invaluable to me in days to come 'cause I had time to go up and take a good look around and ask a lot of questions and get a lot of advice, which many before me were unable to get.

I love you dearly. You are becoming dearer and dearer to me with each passing day because you are so considerate of my folks. Honestly, Sweetheart, my folks praise you to the skies in each letter. Please keep it up, Honey, 'cause the folks are having a pretty rough time, and you and the little guy fill up the void created by mine and Undy's absence.

I love you very much.

The Daddy (Big)

7 March 45

My Dear Little Daddee,

Your Mommy has written me that you are a well-behaved boy, and because of that she and all your Grannies and Aunties and Uncles love you more and more each day. That is really good news and I want you to know that I am very proud of you. Mommy also tells me that because you are so good you are a source of real pleasure to everyone at home. That is good, Daddee.

Please keep it up 'cause Mommy is a bit lonesome without me and I count on you to fill not only your place but also mine in the Mommy's big heart.

Daddee, I want you to do a special favor for me. You know that now that I am away I count on you to take my place at home. Well, Daddee, Easter comes on 1 April this year and I want you to buy some flowers for your Mommy and your two Grannies for me. Please do this 'cause I know it will make them all very happy. That is all for now, Daddee. You keep right on being a good boy and making everyone love you.

Your Daddy

7 March 45

Hello Sweetheart,

Just received another batch of mail yesterday. Believe I have all your letters thru 26 Feb. The airmail letter and the "V" mail note you sent on the 24th both arrived in a dead heat in yesterday afternoon's mail. Try again. Thanks for the pictures. The little guy sure is photogenic. Am returning the Brooklyn pictures to you. Everyone back home has been swell about writing. They all praise my shadow to the sky.

Honey, I could use a large (extra large, you know my fingers) thimble. Sewing is tough without one. Just got thru sewing on a patch. Did as good a job as you ever did, though I'd give a million to have had you around to do it for me.

Sweetheart, don't worry about the little guy's feet. Comes the warm weather have him go around barefoot and have him try to pick up marbles with his little toes. That will strengthen his arch.

Love, Vic

8 March 45
#8

Hello Darling,

Been rather busy today on promotion boards. Trying to get Feldman, Laverty, Kinnear, Lane, Brooks, Miller, and Notto promoted. They all deserve it and I hope they get it. Remetarry too.*

Weather here is just as cool as it was when we arrived. Looking for a change any day now. Should really warm up soon.

We had a little incident in the château. The doggoned thing started up a chimney fire which, had it not been for Sheffey and the boys, would have burned the building right down to the ground. As it was the damage was pretty severe. Thank God my room was untouched so I still live in comfort. Still keeping up my record of a letter a day, which is more than my old lady is doing.

Love,
Vic (Big)

*The names of Eugene Feldman, Douglas Kinnear, Albert Lane, William Brooks, and Claude Miller all appear in the roster of the 50th anniversary edition of *History of the 13th Armored Division*. As noted previously, Feldman was a Major on the Staff of the 46th Tank Battalion. Kinnear, Lane, Brooks, and Miller were First Lieutenants in Companies A, B, and Headquarters of the 46th Tank Battalion. The other names listed in the letter do not appear on the roster, but must have been part of the 46th Tank Battalion if my father was trying to get them promoted.

9 March 45
#9

Hello Sweetheart,

Beautiful day out. Not a cloud in the sky. Hope we get a few more like it. I see by one of your recent letters that you are hungry for a steak. Tough, baby, tough. Why don't you get Sam to get you some steaks from this fellow Jacobs in the packing house on Franklin St. I'm sure he can.

Mommy, everyone writes me about the cute things my shadow does and I must say he is really coming along. However, to me the cutest thing to date is the time he tried to crash the party you and I were having and I had to order him back to bed. Remember how he acted and then finally went back when he saw I meant it. Angon was telling a group of officers at supper last night about the time he saw our shadow jitterbugging in the O's Club at Bowie. Claims it was the funniest thing he ever saw.

Mommy, I love you and the little guy very much.

Vic (Big)

March 10, 1945
#10

Hello Sweetheart,

Received three letters yesterday dated 22, 23, and 25 Feb. Had previously received letters dated 24th and 26th, so I guess we are all caught up. Glad to hear that our stuff arrived. Hope it was all in good shape.

Sweetheart, I hope that you have sent those pictures already 'cause if you are waiting for a request from me to show the post office you certainly aren't thinking. Any letter I've sent you asking about the pictures will do. In any event, I don't think you need a request to send pictures.

The little guy sure must be some character from the tone of the letters about him. I reread all your letters last night. Suggestion: write more about yourself and the little man and what you spend your day doing and less about the weather. I love you both very much.

Vic (Big)

11 March 45
#11

Dearest Catherine,

Received your 28 Feb letter yesterday. Pretty good service. I want the sox in olive drab and they are to be between 91/2" to 10" high from the heel to the top — no higher as they will then come over the top of my shoe.

Can't quite understand this Rachel Samia business*, but as long as she is nice I can't see anything wrong with going with her. What they could want from us in a business way is beyond me.

Hope you had a nice time at my Uncle Ernest's**.

Quit talking about letting me down on the picture deal and get busy and mail them. What are you waiting for? A bawling out or for someone to build a fire under you? Please, honey, I don't understand why you have kept me waiting so long. I thought you'd have them in the mail within a week of the time you got my first letter. Instead all I'm getting is conversation. I'm getting pretty short about it so let's have some action.

I love you.

Vic (Big)

*Rachel Samia, my mother's cousin, sold insurance. What she wanted, and achieved, was to sell my mother a policy.

** My father's uncle, Ernest Abdelnour

12 March 45
#12

Hello Mommy,

I promised Uncle Ernest the pair of high shoes, which I had worn once or twice. The other pair of new ones were to go to my Dad if he wanted them; otherwise save them for me. The low shoes were to go to my family except for the brand new pair, which I want held for me. Hope that is clear.

Nothing new here. Weather warming up. Your mail is coming in regularly. Believe I have all mail you wrote in Feb. Hope you have pictures on the way by now.

War news is fairly good now, but don't get over-optimistic. Be a good while yet for my money. Been keeping pretty busy and am keeping out of mischief, but you know me. Haven't seen a movie since I last saw one with you. We have them but I never seem to be able to get around at the right time.

I love you.

Vic (Big)

13 March 45
#13

Hello Mommy,

Someone is going to have to tell your old man to quit bragging about his kid. Honest, I don't know how people stand me once I get started on the subject of my shadow. Some of the boys brought some nurses out to the château last night. One of them happened to see Ah-Goo's picture (picking flowers). That started me off. I think I bragged too much. Anyhow, the girls didn't seem to mind. Matter of fact, they thought he had rather an impish look in his eyes.

Mommy, I can't even begin to tell you how much time I spend just thinking of you and the shadow. Latest thoughts have been about the day the little guy was born and I got so gloriously drunk. Remember how I came into the hospital about 2200 with some officers who wanted to see him. The Mommy thought I was crazy but let me go on 'cause I was so proud of both of you. That right?

Mommy, how about sending along a couple of bottles of those alka seltzer tablets? I'm pretty near run out.

I love you and my little man very much.

Vic (Big)

14 March 45
#14

Dearest Mommy,

Honey, this evening at 2035 your time and 0135 my time will make it just exactly two months ago that I put you on the train for Brooklyn. I didn't know at that time that I would not see you again for some time, although I had a bit of a suspicion that it might be so. That is why I took a real good look at my Mommy as the train pulled out. I can still remember just how you looked, funny hat and all. You always were beautiful, sweetheart, but somehow or other you looked more beautiful during that last weekend together.

I have missed you as you have missed me, but all in all I am taking it a good deal better than I expected. First two weeks were the worst. Hope you have gotten over the worst part of it by now.

Mommy, that picture (snapshot) you sent me of yourself and Ah-Goo standing in front of our home in Brownwood is a peach. I would like very much to have a colored enlargement (not too large) made of it. Cut out some of the detail so you and he can fill the biggest part of the picture. Hope you understand. I love you both very much.

Vic (Big)

Catherine with Victor, Jr. in Brownwood Texas

CHAPTER *III*

COMBAT

"LIFE IS SO EASY AND GOOD."

On March 15, 1945, the 13th Armored Division began a new phase of their tour of duty in Europe. From that date until early May, the 46th Tank Battalion was almost constantly on the move. For the first few weeks, they were assigned to policing tasks in Germany, such as supervising the movement of displaced persons to DP camps. The ultimate goal was to help force the collapse of the Ruhr Pocket and to forge a path through Germany to the Inn River, which bordered Austria.

On April 10, Task Force Delnore, aided by two tank-infantry teams, received orders to cross the Sieg River at Hennef, where they engaged in their first encounter with enemy fire. Two Americans were killed and 25 were wounded. By the end of the next day, Task Force Delnore had occupied several German villages, including Diessem, Birk, Inger, Algert, and Breidt. They then moved northwest toward Rath, liberating 1,400 Allied prisoners and capturing 70 German soldiers.

On April 13, Task Force Delnore, joined by new reinforcements, spearheaded the movement of the 13th Armored Division across the Wupper River in the Rhine Valley. Reaching the town of Manfort on April 15, they encountered a bridge roadblock over the Dhunn River. In the battle that ensued, the division suffered many casualties. One particularly potent German bullet seriously wounded both the division commander, Major General John Wogan, and the C Company Commander, Captain George Jackson, and also struck my father in the shoulder. In addition to earning the Purple Heart for his battle wound, my father was awarded the Bronze Star for heroic achievement. The Army citation, written by Brig. General Wayland Augur, stated: "Lieutenant Colonel Delnore, disregarding his own wound, and although still under direct sniper fire, administered first aid to the commanding general and supervised his and Captain Jackson's evacuation." In spite of significant losses, the 13th Armored Division succeeded in getting past the roadblock and moved into Leverkusen, where they engaged in a fierce battle that killed Captain Harold Jacobsen.

This bloody victory was soon followed by a much less costly triumph. On April 17, the 46th Tank Battalion's reconnaissance team of 11 men, under my father's personal command, snuck behind enemy lines and seized the German headquarters in Mudlinghoven. They captured two German major generals and their staff, an action which also forced the surrender of 600 German soldiers, thus ending the Battle of the Ruhr. Because the platoon was able to take the Germans totally by surprise, they suffered no casualties. For this mission, Lt. Col. Delnore was awarded the Silver Star, and his 11 reconnaissance soldiers received Bronze Stars. Surely for my father, this mission, which required courage, ingenuity, and stealth, was the highlight of his combat experience.

For the next several days, the men of the 46th Tank Battalion hardly stopped to catch their breath. At Neunkirchen, they repaired their tanks and jeeps, heard Gen. George Patton's address to the 13th Armored Division, and were reassigned to the U.S. Third Army. On April 27, Task Force Delnore crossed the Danube River, then moved 30 miles south to the Isar River. They met with only minor resistance as they marched toward the town of Worth. Here they had the satisfying task of forcing the surrender of many German soldiers, and the even more satisfying job of liberating 400 Allied prisoners of war.

Throughout these dangerous and action-packed weeks, my father continued his daily ritual of making sure that my mother received a letter for every day that he was away. However, even a casual reading of the letters reveals some obvious discrepancies between the life that my father was living and the life that he was writing about. Military censorship, coupled with the determination not to alarm my mother, induced my father to withhold the truth about the dangerous life that he was leading. One obvious example is his letter of April 15, the day that he was wounded in Manfort. He began the letter with the obvious fabrication, "Same old hum-drum life here. Nothing new...", and then went on to observe that "things are really going fine...I am well and happy." He ended the letter with a few complaints about French movies and French cafes! Not only did my father necessarily suppress the truth, but it is also quite certain that he did not write this letter on April 15. It's hard to imagine that while he was fighting in a bloody battle in Germany he took time out to write a letter pretending to be in relaxing in France. Very likely he wrote several letters at one time, filled them with mundane events, postdated them, and mailed them when he had the opportunity.

Another obvious example is a letter dated soon after. Here he expressed his belief that his wife was "still the same good old sweetheart that the Daddy left behind three months ago," guessed that the baby must be keeping her busy, and wistfully wished that he had young Victor with him now. This letter is dated April 17, the day that my father led the daring mission in Mudlinghoven that earned him the Silver Star.

Only later, when military censorship was lifted and combat was over, could my father allude to any of the harrowing events that he and his men were involved in. While the events were actually taking place, the daily letters were filled with nostalgic memories of my parents' courtship, childrearing tips on how best to raise my brother, casual messages from the boys in the unit, ques-

tions about goings on back in Worcester, Easter greetings, descriptions of the spring weather and the beautiful European countryside, and anything else he could think of to assure my mother that everything was fine. Only once, in a letter dated April 22, did my father mention some details concerning Allied troop movements, and he ended with the observation that "if my guessing has been too good, maybe the censor won't pass this."

Two prominent displays of Delnore's Demon Tankers, the nickname of the 46th Tank Battalion

15 March 45
#15

Hello Sweetheart,

Spring must really be here. Hasn't rained in ten days. Weather is beautiful and fairly warm. Roads are all dry and are even getting dusty. On top of the nice weather I really feel fine right now. Just came from a terrific luncheon at the château. What a spread. Won't be able to eat for a week.

Mommy, the more I look at that picture of you and Ah-Goo (taken in front of our home in Brownwood, where you both are smiling so beautifully) the more I fall in love with it. As I asked in my last letter, please have the bulk of the detail cut out, have the picture enlarged, colored, and sent to me. I really love it.

Sweetheart, I hope you play cowboys and crooks with the little guy 'cause he used to love it so much and I know he misses it if you aren't.

Still love you and my little man very much and looking forward to the day when I get back so I can keep on raising both of you right.

Vic (Big)

16 March 45
#16

Hi Honey,

Thinking of you and my shadow last night. Thoughts ran to the first trip we took the little fellow on. It was to Lake Tahoe when he was about two months old. Remember what a nice time we had and how well behaved he was. Honestly, there never was a better baby. He did cry a bit when we left him alone for a while to get some supper, but he sure did snap out of it quickly when we got back.

Augur* was bragging today about how he used to rough his little daughter up (she's a mommy now). He thought that really was something until a couple of the boys told him about what we used to do to the little man. He didn't believe it at first, but when he recalled how he behaved at the O's skit at Bowie, he was ready to believe anything. The old man really thinks a lot of my carbon copy.

I still love you.

Vic (Big)

*Brig. Gen. Wayland B. Augur, assistant 13th Armored Division commanding general

17 March 45
#17

Hello Mommy,

St. Patrick's Day. Hurray for the Irish!

Still reminiscing on the little fellow. Ebert* was telling the boys of the picnic we had at Lake Brownwood and what a beer guzzler the shadow turned out to be. Remember how he passed up the soft drinks for the beer. Does he still like it? Bet you haven't given him any since you got to Worcester. Shame!

*Capt. Henry Ebert, Battalion Motor Officer on the Staff of the 46th Tank Battalion

Had hoped to receive the new pictures by now, but as yet they have not arrived. Awaiting them anxiously.

Sweetheart, you never do tell me what you do with your spare time. You certainly must have some now that your family can help out looking out for my little hero. It was quite a shock to me to hear that you had taken up reading. Never thought it possible. However, one never knows what will happen when one starts getting old. How about keeping up that short-hand and typing?

I love you very much.

Vic (Big)

⁓)⁓

18 March 45
#18

Dearest Catherine,

Received your letter 5 March with the snapshots of the little man. They are very nice. The Mommy looks a good deal thinner. Don't lose too much weight.

Mommy, the only reason I can think of for your not having received my extra long letter with the pictures of the château is that it may be held up by the base censor. Pictures usually are. However, I am sure you will get it shortly as they don't hold them too long. I do hope that you are receiving all my mail. You can tell easily enough because of the dates. I have written you a letter every day since I got to France. Never missed, so help me. Can't say as much for the Mommy, can we?

Nothing new. Life is really comfortable so far. Never as rough as it was back in the States when we were on maneuvers. I do hope those pictures are on the way by now. I'll take the 5 x 7 pictures as well as the 2 x 3 . I have a place to carry them.

I love you very much.

Vic (Big)

Catherine with Victor, Jr. in Worcester, Massachusetts, where they lived during my father's absence

19 March 45

My Most Dear Mommy,

This is going to be a fairly hard letter to write 'cause I have nothing new to say, but I do feel that I must keep up my record of writing to my little family every day. I want you both to know that the daddy is healthy, warm, comfortable, well fed, and well clothed. Just as well as I have ever been. Outside of not having my little family with me, I have about everything I want.

The boys are all well and I still have them all with me just as when we left. They are all well behaved and are no trouble at all. In fact, as usual, our outfit has been doing better than the others. Guess that is getting to be a pretty old story around the division. Cech* in particular has grown up somewhat. Henry showed me some pictures of his baby. She is cute. Too bad he couldn't have seen her.

I hope that the war bonds have started to come in by now. Let me know. I love you.

Vic (Big)

*1 Lt. Victor Cech, Reconnaissance Officer on the Staff of the 46th Tank Battalion

20 March 45
#20

Hello Mommy,

Hope you and the little fellow are used to the New England cold by now. It certainly was cold there at the time of my last visit. When I think about it, I wonder how we used to stand it. Weather in this part of Europe is certainly much more pleasant. It has not rained in more than three weeks. Spring certainly is in the air. Farmers plowing their fields, etc. I haven't had to wear my long johns yet. Don't expect to have to either. Still getting well fed and well taken care of. I don't know how it's done, but they sure do give us good chow over here.

Haven't bumped into anyone from home that we know yet. Guess too many of them are in rear echelon troops, QM*, etc. I love you and my little fellow very much and do think of both of you constantly, as I know you do of me. Can you follow that ok?

Vic (Big)

*Quartermaster Corps, the branch of the U.S. Army responsible for food, clothing, and equipment

21 March 45
#21

Dearest Mommy,

Shouldn't have bragged about the weather in my last letter 'cause it sure is raining today. However, it looks like it might clear up and anyway it was getting too dusty. Mommy, I haven't had but one letter from you in a week. I know it is not your fault 'cause that is the way mail comes in. I mention this only 'cause you may have asked some questions in your letters which I am not answering in mine. Be patient, honey.

I sure do miss my little man, although not as much as I feared I might. He's a regular topic of conversation around headquarters. Everyone brags about him. He made quite a name for himself.

Expecting a big batch of mail this pm. I hope that the pictures of you and Ah-Goo are in it.

Love,
Vic (Big)

22 March 45
#22

Hello Sweetheart,

Just think, our little fellow was 20 months old day before yesterday. He must be quite a man by now, Mommy. From the tone of your letters, he must be getting to be a bit on the devilish side. Does he still row his boat? Play cowboys and crooks? Still ask for cookie? How about piggy-back rides? Are you giving him any? I sure hope you are, Mommy, 'cause you know how he enjoyed all those things. How about beer? Giving him any? I'll bet not. Catherine, don't you let anyone tell you how to raise him. You keep right on with him exactly as we used to. I think we were doing pretty good.

That stroller looks practical, but a bit on the girlie side. I was explaining to the little fellow that the Daddy was going away, that he was now head of the family, and that I expected him to look after and take care of the Mommy while the Daddy was away. He looked all mixed up.

I love you.

Vic (Big)

23 March 45
#23

Hello Sweetheart,

Your mail is starting to come in again. Very happy to hear that Ed Ghiz is back and in good health. It's about time he got around to marrying Evelyn Kouri*. If he had some sense, he would have married her long ago. She's my favorite on the hill next to you, as you probably already know.

Sweetheart, don't ever worry about the chow we eat. It's way better than in the States. Just as fancy and more. On trips I carry my own, but I have never eaten them, as I just invite myself into someone's mess and that is the end of that. Everyone is glad to have you eat with them.

What is this I hear about the shadow getting fresh? Better stop it, Mommy, or you'll be sorry later. Raise him your own way. Don't listen to the old folks. Times change.

I love you and the little daddee very much.

Vic (Big)

*Ed Ghiz and Evelyn Kouri were childhood friends of my parents. During World War II, Ed was in the Army, and was in combat in the China-Burma-India theater. Ed was also the brother of Bill Ghiz, who figures importantly in the next chapter.

23 March 45

On an embossed card titled EASTER GREET-INGS FROM FRANCE, Thirteenth Ar-mored Division, A.P.O. 263 C/O Post-master, New York, N.Y. my father sent the following "pre-written" card. The only original portions of the card were the penned in names "Catherine and Vic-tor" and the signature "Vic," followed by a brief message to "Wish your folks a Happy Easter for me."

EASTER GREETINGS

FROM

FRANCE

THIRTEENTH ARMORED DIVISION
A. P. O. 263 C/O POSTMASTER
NEW YORK, N. Y.

Dear Catherine and Victor,

Over the miles that separate us from cherished homes and dear ones this Easter Message wings its way.

In far off France, the land of towering Cathedrals and ancient Churches, our Catholic chaplains will fold your names in prayer. Along with them I will be thinking of you as the Communion bell rings, for I know that is when you will be thinking most of me.

Until the dawn of a new and lasting Peace in Christ, may God be with you, and Mary, our Lady of the Resurrection, protect you each anxious hour:

Vic

Wish your folks a happy Easter for me.

24 March 45
#24

Hello Sweetheart,

I have mailed you two packages. One, a box, contains two German machine guns, the other, a cylinder, contains a German rifle. The weapons are packed in grease and are in a state of disassembly, so I suggest you don't unpack them. Course, if Sam or Al* think they can put them together and want to take on the job of cleaning them once a week, go ahead and let them unpack them. They can't hurt them as long as they don't allow them to get rusty.

Weather is sure beautiful here. Hope it holds out thru Easter Sunday. Trees are beginning to bud.

Hope you and the family received the Easter card greeting I sent you. Personally, I didn't like the message. It sounded too artificial and flowery. However, it was all that was available. I'd like very much to have a snapshot of my little family taken in their Easter finery. Hope you thought of buying yourself a new Easter outfit.

Love, Vic (Big)

*two of my mother's brothers, Samuel and Albert Abdelmaseh

25 March 45
#25

My Dearest Wife,

I'm particularly happy today because I received 7 letters from you dated anywhere from 1 March to 15 March. They were really wonderful to read. Mommy, please do exactly as the doctor asked as regards Victor's feet. It is really important. No matter what anyone tells you and no matter how grotesque the shoes may look on his feet, you do it.

Sweetheart, I get a real kick out of the self-satisfaction you get from showing, I was going to say throwing, my rank around. You never acted very proud of it when I was with you. Heck, you took my promotion announcements as commonplace things. Remember! How come you're so proud all of a sudden? To be truthful, I'm vain enough to like your sudden appreciation.

I love you.

Vic (Big)

26 March 45
#26

Hello Mommy,

I reread your seven letters again and again. Sure made nice reading. Mommy, the daddy is going to wring your little neck. When I wrote you about the socks, I told you the exact color and size and you've asked me about them twice since. Of course, olive drab, what else? Come on, honey, wake up.

Mommy, I didn't mean for you to think that 'cause I wanted the socks, I expected this mess to continue 'cause it isn't. Hell, the Krauts are running like hell. Very little fight left in them. I bet it's all over in less than three months. Possible chance three weeks. That make you feel better?

I love you more than I can put into words, and just 'cause I don't say I miss you doesn't mean I don't. It's just that I'd rather not think or write about it. I love you.

Vic (Big)

27 March 45
#27

Dearest Mommy,

That gal Nicole you act so jealous over is the blonde who lived at our château. I explained all about her in my long letter, which is obviously being held up for censorship due to the postcards enclosed. I hope you get the letter soon. If you don't, don't get excited as there wasn't anything awfully good in the letter. It just described where and with whom we lived.

Sweetheart, I hope you take warning from Barbara Salem's and Johnny David's wife's* appearance and not let yourself get in the same fix. You did slip for a while, but you came out of it pretty well this winter. Please, Mommy, 'cause I think you are so beautiful and I would like to have you remain so.

Glad to hear that my little man is so well behaved. Hope he keeps it up. I love you both very much.

Vic (Big)

*friends from Worcester

28 March 45
#28

Dearest Mommy,

Your mail is in one of those slumps now. Haven't received any for 5 days. Expect it to come in in one big batch. Now that Easter is almost upon us, I keep thinking of how you'll look with your new Easter outfit, which I hope you had good sense enough to buy.

Ah-Goo ought to put in quite an appearance too. You must have had to buy him all new stuff now that he has outgrown all his old stuff. Say, Pal, don't think that just because I don't paragraph my letters that I have forgotten that I am supposed to. I use this system to save space*.

To get back to Easter outfits, I'll be wearing the same clothes that the rest of the Army is wearing, so I won't send you a picture, but I do hope that you send me one of you and the shadow.

Love,
Vic (Big)

*In fact, the reader will note that for this book all the letters have been organized into paragraphs.

29 March 45
#29

My Dearest Mommy,

Good weather lately. Getting more beautiful every day. Trees are budding. Spring is really here. Thank God, although it hasn't been a tough winter so far. Today is Holy Thursday, and it looks like this is going to be a really nice Easter.

The war situation looks really good. Probably a lot better than the radio broadcasts are putting out due to security. Anyhow, Mommy, I'll go on record that the Germans quit by my birthday *, and if I get odds I'd say even before then. When they quit, they'll quit. None of this guerilla fighting you've been reading about. Heck, the Germans are too orderly and too used to taking orders. When they quit it will be final and complete. That make you feel better?

I love you and think of you constantly.

Vic (Big)

*June 27

30 March 45
#30

My Most Dear Mommy,

Good Friday. Bet you are happy Lent is over. I know I always used to be. Your mail still hasn't come in, but I just keep thinking of how nice it will be to read it all at once when it does.

Mommy, I've seen some of the European trailers here. Compared to ours*, they are a bunch of junk. They are wagon type. Look like gypsy wagons. However, seeing them brought to mind our old trailer and the happy and somewhat crazy times we had in it. Remember the time we had fourteen people in the doggone old thing. Wouldn't have believed it possible to look at the size of the thing. I was always worried about how you would take it when we sold the trailer. Needless to say, you took it way better than I expected you to.

All my love. Happy Easter.

Vic (Big)

*In the early years of their marriage, my parents lived in a trailer, which they sold when they left Camp Bowie, Texas.

31 March 45
#31

My Dearest Most Sweet Mommy,

You've made the Daddy's Easter holiday a most happy one. Yesterday I received five letters from you, including one letter mailed as late as 25 March. Unbelievable! The pictures were included and they were most beautiful. My shadow sure has taken on a lot of weight. He sure does look good and healthy. The Mommy looks as beautiful as ever. Even got a mischievous twinkle in her eye. The news from you is all good. Heck, you even received my long letter. Wasn't much to it, was there?

I do hope that you all feel as optimistic about the war situation as I do. Honestly, it is really good. Heck, I'm beginning to get my peacetime uniforms in shape.

I hope you and your entire family have a most enjoyable Easter tomorrow. I'll be thinking of you.

Love,
Vic (Big)

1 April 45
#1

Happy Easter, Mommy.

I do hope that my little family and all the folks back home do have a very happy one, and I hope we are all united for the next one. Did you and Ah-Goo's two Grannies like the flowers he sent you?

Mommy, it is so hard to realize that a war is going on. It's so beautiful and so peaceful out. Church bells are ringing all over the place. I intend going to mass at 11:30. We've taken over the local church for a very special Easter service. I'll be thinking of my little family and all the folks back home all through the service.

I want you and Ah-Goo to know that I do miss you both very much today and am looking forward to being with you next Easter.

I love you.

Easter Sunday on the battlefront

Vic (Big)

2 April 45
#2

Dearest Mommy,

I've been reading in the papers that you are getting some really nice weather home. I'm sure happy for you 'cause I know how you dislike the cold. Weather here turned cold and rainy today. Funny thing, although the weather never seems really cold, there is very little difference in the temperature now and 2 months ago. I wear exactly the same clothes.

Leaves are all out now and it is turning more beautiful than ever. Honestly, honey, you have no idea of how much more beautiful the countryside in Europe is than in America. There are little or no wild woods. All fields are beautiful. No underbrush anywhere. Grass is always green even in winter and it is everywhere. Trees are extremely tall. Most look like they have been planted even in woods 'cause they are in even rows. More later.

I love you.

Vic (Big)

3 April 45
#3

Dearest Mommy,

I guess the reason the country here is more beautiful is chiefly because it is older, that is, man has had a longer period of time to beautify it. It sure is pretty. Makes the U.S., except New England down through Pennsylvania, look sick. Even then it is much prettier than that area.

The towns are not as pretty as ours. Whereas our houses are set back from the street, theirs are flush with little or no sidewalks except in large cities. In America our farmers build their homes on their farmland. Here the farmers build their homes together to make small villages. Their farms radiate out from the villages. Makes the country far prettier, but the towns stink, and I mean stink, not smell. However, the slightly larger villages are not so bad. I hope I haven't bored you.

I love you very much.

Vic (Big)

4 April 45
#4

Hello Sweetheart,

Received quite a bit of mail yesterday. One from you giving Pete's address*. One from my folks dated 14 March, and one from Naj mailed the 9th of March. When you recall that a week ago I received a letter from you postmarked 25 March, you get a pretty good idea of how erratic the mail service is.

---

*My mother's brother, Peter Abdelmaseh, had enlisted in the Navy and was stationed in the South Pacific.

Very happy to hear that Ah-Goo is an outdoor boy, but don't like the idea of your having to bribe him to come in. You never used to have to bribe him. How come you have to now? Getting spoiled?

I haven't received your package as yet, but expect it any day now. Got the letter in which you tell of the mailman asking me not to type the address. Had those already made up. They look discernible enough. Let me know if he still complains.

I love you.

Vic (Big)

5 April 45
#5

Dearest Mommy,

If you worked for me I'd fire you. Sweetheart, take care of that birth certificate thing. I don't know why you should ask me if it is OK to go ahead. Get the doggoned thing. I don't understand your reference to Spanish Town. Please clarify.

I've been getting all kinds of mail and from everyone back home. It is very nice to be remembered. Received an exceptionally long letter from Vicki*. She plans on coming home about 1 May. I'd like to be there when my two namesakes meet. I'll bet it is a three ring circus.

Boys here are all fine and send their love. Ebert sends special carload. Sheffey says he can spare a bit too. Feldman sends all his to Victor. I love the Mommy.

Vic (Big)

---

*My father's sister, Victoria Stevens, lived in Los Angeles. Like him, Vicki had an infant son named Victor. Apparently it did not occur to my father that nephew Victor might have been named after his mother, rather than after his uncle.

[undated]

Hello Sweetheart*,

Received that swell letter from you and think you are swell to remember a bald-headed old man like me. But then, if I remember correctly, you were my first girl, so why shouldn't you remember?

From your letter I gather that you like my little fellow almost as much as you like me (more?). Can't say that I blame you 'cause he certainly is a three ring circus if ever there was one.

Rachel, honey, I do hope that you aren't allowing that married sister of yours to stick around the house like an old woman. Please don't allow her to if she is. Hell, she is too young and there is too much going on. Do me a favor and drag her out. Remember one thing, though, don't let her date sailors. You can't trust them.

Vic

* "Sweetheart" in this letter is my mother's younger sister, Rachel Abdelmaseh, who, along with my mother and brother, lived in the Worcester home of her parents. Although the exact date of the letter is unknown, it was probably written in early April. The salutation attests to the close relationship between my father and his young sister-in-law.

6 April 45
#6

Hello Sweetheart,

Received your 11 March letter. All my nurse pals were gone when I got back to the château, but I wasted no time getting myself a few more. Nice kids but oh how lonesome and disillusioned. Never complain though.

How did Hep* act at the wedding? I bet he too was nervous? Glad to hear that Victor behaved so well at your folks' church. Maybe he was cut out to be an Orthodox**.

Please explain once again to the folks that the mail situation just can't be helped and that I do write them at least once a week. It's amazing that the mail service is as good as it is.

I love you more and more each day 'cause I realize what a big place you filled in my heart.

I love you.

Vic (Big)

*Ed Ghiz's nickname

**My mother was brought up in the Syrian Orthodox Church and converted to Roman Catholicism when she married my father. The wedding of Ed Ghiz and Evelyn Kouri took place in the Orthodox Church.

7 April 45
#7

Dearest Mommy,

Thank God the weather has cleared up and warmed up somewhat. Had a three-day spell of tough weather. Mommy, I do hope that you aren't becoming an old stay at home. Please, honey, I want you to enjoy yourself. I trust you implicitly and I do want you to amuse yourself.

I've been having a fairly good time here, although amusement and entertainment as we know them at home are practically nonexistent. No restaurant open to us, no dances, no parties other than those we contrive with nurses. Films are few and far between but of good quality. However, with all that we manage to have a pretty good time with the boys all together, playing cards, just conversation, etc., over bottles of "liberated" wine and champagne.

I love you.

Vic (Big)

8 April 45
#8

Hello Sweetheart,

Sunday and a beautiful day. Just had a steak dinner and feeling well. Had a really hot bath last night followed by ten hours good sleep. Got up at 0930 and went to church at 1030, then dinner. It is now 1230. You are still in bed at home, it being 0630 there. There is six hours difference in our time now since we went on War Time last Sunday. You may have too. If so we are still 5 hours in difference. Let me know.

Have lost hardly any weight yet 'cause life is so easy and good. Chow best I have ever seen in the Army. To date I've slept in as good a bed as I have at home all but about 10 nights. So quit worrying about the tough life you think I'm leading 'cause it ain't so. Outside of not having my family with me, everything is perfect. I still have the same gang I left the States with. May lose John Biddle* though. He has an infection in his eye. Hope to get him back though.

I love you and the shadow very much.

Vic (Big)

*Capt. John Biddle, Battalion Surgeon on the Staff of the 46th Tank Battalion

9 April 45
#9

Hello Sweetheart,

Still love you and the little guy very much. Been thinking back on our life together quite a bit of late. You know, honey, it's funny but I can remember the pleasant incidents only. You and I have had quite a few squabbles same as most married folks, but I really have to rack my brain to remember any of them, whereas the pleasant incidents come to mind quite readily.

I still remember vividly the first date we had (you talked me into it, remember?). Unlike most men, I can even remember the dress you wore. How's that? You wore a white dress with a very large flower design. Flower was reddish with black shading. Am I wrong, honey? Anyhow, I laugh every time I think of how sophisticated you tried to act. Wanted to smoke and ordered a scotch and soda. Phooey! Then, to top it all off, remember how you refused to go home. Boy, was I scared of your mother after bringing you in so late.

I love you.

Vic (Big)

10 April 45
#10

Dearest Mommy,

Sure do love the Mommy very much. I spend a good deal of my time thinking, or rather, reviewing the good times we used to have together. Got to thinking last night about the time you proposed to me. Pardon me! I mean I proposed to you.

Remember the old tin Lizzie the Daddy used to take the Mommy out with? It may have been just a heap of junk to some people, but it was the Daddy's chief means of having dates with the mommy. Well, Mommy, remember how I cussed that day 'cause the doggoned thing had gotten stuck and then at the end of all those cuss words I blurted out the proposal. That really was something. Guess you'll never forget it.

In case you have, date was 5 July, 1938. Right?

Love,
Vic (Big)

11 April 45
#11

Dearest Sweetheart,

Still reminiscing. Mommy, remember the time I took you out to the Red Roof on a Saturday night? It was the first time we had gone to the place. We had a pretty good time, but it was a bit close when we found that they had a cover charge and that I had just ten cents more. Pretty embarrassing, but the Mommy was awfully nice about it and didn't make the Daddy feel too bad about it. Come to think of it, we never did go back to the place. I often wonder why 'cause it was nice enough.

Mail hasn't caught up with me lately, so I can't answer any specific questions you may be asking.

I love you.

Vic (Big)

12 April 45
#12

Dearest Sweetheart,

I miss the little man very much. I do enjoy reading about his antics in your and the family's letters. You know how much fun the Daddy used to have with the Daddee. Boy, I'd give ten years of my life to be able to stay with my little family. I really do love you both, as you well know.

I miss you more than I can tell, but not in the way I thought I would. I got used to that in about three weeks. I just miss having you around to boss and educate. You know how I love to nag you. I miss those lazy Sundays when I used to just sit around and listen to the radio. I miss all the things I used to do with you. I look forward to taking them up again. The sooner the better.

Vic (Big)

13 April 45
#13

Dear, dear Mommy,

You know, Sweetheart, my French is getting real good. I can parlay it like nobody's business. Most of the boys use the Brail system*, but I find you do better if you can speak their language. Not that the Daddy hasn't been a good boy, 'cause I can assure you he has been as good a boy as he ever was when he was home. Figure that one out if you can. Ha-ha!

Seriously though, Sweetheart, I do feel sorry for the French people, but gosh they are inefficient, even more so than you. I guess I'm giving you a bad time in this letter. I don't mean to, honey, 'cause I love you more than anyone else in this world.

Vic (Big)

*Probably my father confused Braille, the system by which blind people can read, with sign language, the system of hand gestures by which some deaf people communicate. As any foreign traveler with limited knowledge of the native language knows, hand gestures are a very useful and effective way of communicating. Most certainly, American GI's who wanted to communicate with the French became fluent in their own version of sign language.

14 April 45

Dearest Mommy,

Here it is now three months separated, but it sure looks as though this war is really folding up, and I mean in a hurry. Received the news of President Roosevelt's death* yesterday. Sure is a shock to our troops, who really think the world of him.

*FDR died of a stroke on April 12, 1945.

It's hard to realize that we have been separated for as long as we have, but, Sweetheart, the future sure does look bright.

Mail has been lousy lately. Have received nothing for a week, but am looking forward anxiously to reading a huge batch when it comes in.

All my boys are well and happy and send their love to you. I love you and my shadow very much.

Vic (Big)

15 April 45
#15

Hello Sweetheart,

Same old hum-drum life here. Nothing new. Haven't seen a good movie but one since I left home and you. However, things are really going fine, and I want you to know that I am well and happy. You know, Sweetheart, no one appreciates the good old U.S. until they leave it.

Europe, as I have told you, is much more picturesque and way much more beautiful. However, what people do for amusement I'll never know. France has some picture houses, but the French films I hear are no good, and what would a Frenchman want with an English dialogue movie? Cafes are numerous but small and dirty, and the stuff they put out — poison. However, it is not as bad as the Daddy expected. You might even say the Daddy is enjoying himself.

I love you.

Vic (Big)

HOW MY FATHER REALLY SPENT APRIL 15, 1945:

THE UNITED STATES OF AMERICA

TO ALL WHO SHALL SEE THESE PRESENTS, GREETING:

THIS IS TO CERTIFY THAT
THE PRESIDENT OF THE UNITED STATES OF AMERICA
AUTHORIZED BY ORDER OF
GENERAL GEORGE WASHINGTON, AUGUST 7, 1782
HAS AWARDED

THE PURPLE HEART

TO

Lieutenant Colonel Victor E. Delnore, 032 398, Infantry

FOR

WOUNDS RECEIVED IN ACTION

European Theater of Operations, 15 April 1945

GIVEN UNDER MY HAND IN THE CITY OF WASHINGTON
THIS   18th   DAY OF   August   19 49

MAJOR GENERAL
THE ADJUTANT GENERAL

SECRETARY OF ▮▮▮ THE ARMY

THE UNITED STATES OF AMERICA

TO ALL WHO SHALL SEE THESE PRESENTS, GREETING:

THIS IS TO CERTIFY THAT
THE PRESIDENT OF THE UNITED STATES OF AMERICA
AUTHORIZED BY EXECUTIVE ORDER, FEBRUARY 4, 1944
HAS AWARDED

THE BRONZE STAR MEDAL

TO

Lieutenant Colonel Victor E. Delnore, 032 398, Infantry

FOR

HEROISM IN GROUND COMBAT

near Manfort, Germany, 15 April 1945

GIVEN UNDER MY HAND IN THE CITY OF WASHINGTON
THIS   18th   DAY OF   August   19 49

MAJOR GENERAL
THE ADJUTANT GENERAL

SECRETARY OF ▮▮▮ THE ARMY

HEADQUARTERS
13TH ARMORED DIVISION
CAMP COOKE, CALIFORNIA

C I T A T I O N

For Award of The

BRONZE STAR MEDAL

VICTOR E. DELNORE, O 337 481, Lieutenant Colonel, Infantry, Headquarters 46th Tank Battalion, for heroic achievement in connection with military operations against an enemy of the United States on 15 April 1945, in the vicinity of Manfort, Germany. While supervising operations of an element of his task force against an enemy road block, Lieutenant Colonel Delnore observed Major General Wogan, Division Commander, exposed unknowingly to enemy fire. Disregarding his own safety, Lieutenant Colonel Delnore brought General Wogan to comparative safety in a near-by ditch. While observing from the ditch, General Wogan, Lieutenant Colonel Delnore and Captain Jackson (Company C, 46th Tank Battalion) were hit by sniper fire. Lieutenant Colonel Delnore, disregarding his own wound, and although still under direct sniper fire, administered first aid to the Commanding General and supervised his and Captain Jackson's evacuation. Lieutenant Colonel Delnore's actions were in keeping with the highest traditions of the military service. Entered military service from Worcester, Massachusetts.

WAYLAND B. AUGUR
Brigadier General, U. S. Army
Commanding

Professional sketch of the April 15 battle at the Dhunn River, found among my father's papers after his death

This long shot of the Dhunn River in Manfort, Germany shows the bridge that was blocked by the Germans in April 1945. In the battle that ensued, the 13th Armored Division suffered many casualties. My father's descriptive label on the original photo states: "Bridge as seen looking west from autobahn; wounded on south (left) bank." This photo, as well as the one on the next page, was taken by my father during a family trip through Germany in 1954.

The photo of my mother, brother, sister and me places us on the exact spot where my father and his comrades were shot. Note the house and bushes in the background, which can be seen at the far left in the photo of the Dhunn River (see preceding page). My father labeled this photo: "6 Sept. 54, Leverkusen, exact spot at which wounded 15 Apr. 45."

16 April 45
#16

Hello Sweetheart,

Doggone it! All the nurses are gone. Now the Daddy has to really go hunting. It's a shame 'cause he was getting along real good with the nurses. Oh well, it will keep me young and aggressive to have to chase the young girls.

Sometimes I wonder how they put up with me 'cause about all I do is show pictures of you and Victor and talk about both of you all thru the evenings. Girls seem to enjoy listening. Think I'm different. But now they are gone and the Daddy is unhappy and will miss the Mommy more than ever. Hope they send a new batch in, but I don't think so.

I love you.

Vic (Big)

17 April 45
#17

Hello Mommy,

How is the Mommy doing these days? I bet she is still the same good old sweetheart that the Daddy left behind three months ago. I do hope that you don't miss him too much and that you are keeping yourself busy. I guess with Ah-Goo you must be kept pretty busy. There is a prize package!

As you know, I sure had a lot of fun with him. I do wish I had him with me ~~know~~ now. I really despair these months that I will never be able to replace ~~those months~~. Excuse the errors. I'm trying to listen to the news and write this letter at the same time.

I love you.

Vic (Big)

WHAT REALLY HAPPENED ON APRIL 17, 1945:

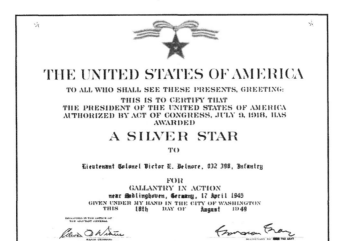

THE UNITED STATES OF AMERICA

TO ALL WHO SHALL SEE THESE PRESENTS, GREETING:

THIS IS TO CERTIFY THAT
THE PRESIDENT OF THE UNITED STATES OF AMERICA
AUTHORIZED BY ACT OF CONGRESS, JULY 9, 1918, HAS
AWARDED

A SILVER STAR

TO

Lieutenant Colonel Victor E. Delnore, 032 398, Infantry

FOR
GALLANTRY IN ACTION
near Mudlinghoven, Germany, 17 April 1945
GIVEN UNDER MY HAND IN THE CITY OF WASHINGTON
THIS   18th   DAY OF   August   1949

HEADQUARTERS 13TH ARMORED DIVISION
APO 263   U. S. ARMY

11 May 1945

C I T A T I O N

For Award of The

SILVER STAR

VICTOR E. DELNORE, O 337 481, Lieutenant Colonel, Infantry, Headquarters 46th Tank Battalion, for gallantry in action on 17 April 1945
in the vicinity of Mudlinghoven, Germany. Apprised of a possible enemy
headquarters for anti-aircraft units, Lieutenant Colonel Delnore organized a volunteer commando task force from his Reconnaissance Platoon and
advanced rapidly across open terrain. He evaded German 88mm fire from
the woods to the east by heading toward a draw northwest of hostile guns.
Encountering small arms fire, Lieutenant Colonel Delnore regrouped his
men, minus supporting troops, and made a run for the enemy Command Post.
Surprise was so great that the surrender of two Major Generals and 600
German flak troops was effected without a single American casualty. This
officer's bravery, skill and exceptional devotion to duty reflect high
credit upon himself and the Army. Entered military service from Worcester,
Massachusetts.

JOHN MILLIKIN
Major General, U. S. Army
Commanding

18 April 45
#18

Hello Sweetheart,

You know, it's really funny that all the time I have been overseas and with all the traveling I have done, I never ran into anyone from the hill. Yet I run into so many people I knew back in the States. Guess most of the boys from the hill are in the QM or something like that. Seems so from the addresses in the *St. George's Journal**.

Your package with the leather case for the pictures has not arrived yet. Believe you mailed it a month ago. This mail service sure is screwy. On the 29th of March I received a letter dated and mailed the 25th. Here it is three weeks later and that is still the latest written letter that I have received. Sure is sporadic.

I love you.

Vic (Big)

*newsletter published by St. George's Church in Worcester

19 April 45
#19

Hello Mommy,

Well, I finally did receive some mail. Your letters of the 26th, 27th, and 28th came in today. Still no sign of the package. Very pleasant to hear from you. Ah-Goo must be getting to be quite a lad. His vocabulary sure has grown. He'll be making passes at the girls soon.

The war news sure is good. The war should be about over here by the time you receive this letter. That is except for the little mopping up which remains to be done. Same as the Ruhr pocket. Boy, that will be a day. You have absolutely no idea how rough it is on civilians over here.

I love you.

Vic (Big)

20 April 45
#20

Hello Sweetheart,

Here it is the little fellow's birthday again. Let's see, he is now 21 months old. According to your last letter, he is 1 1/2" taller and five pounds heavier. His weight really showed up on him in those colored pictures you took. He looks really healthy, which means that the Mommy has been taking good care of the little Daddee for the big Daddy.

Bless you. I sure wish we had had him sooner. You'll never know how much happiness he has brought into my life. I look forward to being with both of you again in the not too far future.

I do love you.

Vic (Big)

21 April 45
#21

Dearest Mommy,

Received two letters from you today, and it sure makes me feel good. One of your letters hurt me somewhat. What do you mean by that crack that I probably didn't write you on the 6th? I did, hon. It must be delayed due to censorship.

Doggone this European weather. Here you are talking about temperatures up in the 80's, and I don't notice a difference of 10% between now and the time we arrived. Trees are all broken out and it's spring OK, but no feeling of warmth yet. Hope it comes soon 'cause it sure is chilly nights.

I love you.

Vic (Big)

22 April 45
#22

Hello Mommy,

Received two more very welcome letters from you today. This doggoned war is over over here, but these damned fool Germans have absolutely no control over their government.

From now on, here is what should happen. Within 10 days we should make a juncture with Russian troops in at least three places, splitting German defenses into three pockets. One north of Berlin, one in the Czech mountains, and one in the Austrian Alps south of the Danube. From there on it will be a mop up detail same as the Ruhr pocket, but more fierce. The Austrian Alps sector will be where we will catch all the die-hards.

If my guessing has been too good, maybe the censor won't pass this.

I love you.

Vic (Big)

23 April 45
#23

Dearest Mommy,

Received a huge batch of mail from home today. Letters from you thru 10 April, couple from the folks, couple from Najla, one from Ed Ghiz mailed from CBI*. Can't answer Ed's 'cause his address no longer applies. Please call them up and tell them I received his letter and that I wish them all kinds of luck.

You don't know how welcome this batch of mail has been, Mommy. Here's why. The Daddy took to bed yesterday with the grippe, running a fever of 103.8. Felt miserable. Fever cracked today down to 101. Ought to be up and around in a couple of days. Come hell or high water, the mail goes out to Mommy. Now how do you feel about missing writing once in a while?

I love you.

Vic (Big)

*China-Burma-India theater

24 April 45
#24

Hello Sweetheart,

Still in bed, but feel a whole lot better. Waiting on the doc to show up and give me the OK on getting up. No matter what anyone says, though, I'm spending the rest of this day in bed. Heck, weather is miserable out. Rain, hail, etc. Whole world has gone crazy.

Glad to see you've found a house you like. I aim to please the Mommy. Forget about the fish pole. I'm no fisherman anyway. I still might become one if you would do your job as a faithful wife should and clean up the mess of fish I bring home. That one time you refused to clean that 15 pounder I brought home was too much for me. No matter what, I still love you.

Vic (Big)

25 April 45
#25

Hello Darling,

Well, the Daddy is out of bed once again, and is going around making just as much noise as ever. I have reread that huge batch of mail that I have been receiving for the past four days. It makes wonderful reading. That is, when I can understand it. The Mommy had better go back to school. Her use of grammar and phrasing of sentences is just too awful to let go by. Better reread what you write and you'll see what I mean. You're plain careless, but don't get angry and quit writing. I just want you to be a better example to my shadow. Anyhow, honey, these letters are full of news of my little man, which is what I want to read about.

I love you very much.

Vic (Big)

26 April 45
#26

Honey,

Received your 15 April letter, in which you tell of Victor's illness. Thank God he is over it. There is no point in bawling you out, though I feel like it, so I'll pass the incident off with this one remark, which I hope you fix indelibly in your mind. UNTIL OUR LITTLE FELLOW LEARNS TO EXPRESS HIMSELF INTELLIGENTLY, EVERY ACHE OR PAIN, CAUSE OF WHICH IS UNDETERMINED, WILL BE CHECKED BY A PHYSICIAN. Now Sweetheart, please don't break that rule or we'll be without our little fellow 'cause he can't tell us what is wrong.

I had the same sickness the week of Jan 24th, 1932. Kept me out of school two weeks. Lost 14 lbs. Every time I get a cold now, my left eardrum still bothers me slightly (tickles). Sickness caused by sore throat spreading thru Eustachian tubes into inner ear. What makes it dangerous is proximity of infection to brain, and it is dangerous.

Love,
Vic (Big)

27 April 45
#27

Hello Mommy,

To date I have received none of your packages. I guess it takes about two months to get here. I hope that Ah-Goo had no aftereffects from his illness. If so, let me know. Did the doc have you drop some mercurochrome into his ear while it was running? It takes the odor out of the discharge.

I hear the Mommy is losing some weight. Swell, but don't you dare go below 120 lbs. Everyone tells me I've lost weight. I don't feel it. Been eating regular and living easy, so no reason for it.

Received that batch of pictures of you and Ah-Goo. He looks a bit small yet to be escorting you around, but I guess he'll grow into the job in due time. Mommy takes a much nicer picture when she doesn't set her face for the camera. Smile.

Love,
Vic (Big)

28 April 45
#28

Hello Mommy,

Still haven't received those packages from home yet. However, that batch of mail I received sure was nice to have. The part about the mail I really enjoyed was the fact that there was so much news of my shadow. I can't even begin to tell you how much time I spend just thinking of you and him. Please keep up the good work in your letters.

Weather here has been cold and rainy for 10 days now. So help me, I can't understand this weather they have here. The winter was so mild, yet real spring never seems to come. I actually am wearing more clothes than I did on 1 Feb.

I love you.

Vic (Big)

29 April 45
#29

Hello Sweetheart,

At last I've bumped into a couple of guys from Worcester. Saw a large 10-ton truck with "Worcester, Mass" painted on the front bumper. The driver turned out to be an Italian boy from Hamilton St. who knew me, but I couldn't place him. I forget his name now (you know, I must be getting old), but it was something like Salerno. We had a nice little chat and then parted.

Ran into another boy named Reynolds from Elm St. He'd been a prisoner of the Germans, who had been liberated. Didn't know me, and I didn't know him, but we had a little bull session. I don't know why, but I never do run into anyone from the hill. Well, I may some day.

I love you.

Vic (Big)

30 April 45
#30

Dearest Mommy,

I think you are cute. Here you are trying out the different ways of getting mail to me. Sweetheart, your best bet is just any kind of mail. It makes absolutely no difference how you mail it 'cause the problem is in the shipping. First means available is the way it goes. You can't compare my mail to you with your mail to me, as that is no problem because there is no lack of space.

Sooo! You just keep writing no matter how and quit worrying your pretty little head about it getting to the Daddy. It makes no difference. OK now?

I've been trying to get some news on Undy, but it is an impossible situation at the present time.

I love you.

Vic (Big)

1 May 45
#1

Hello Sweetheart,

This damned war is over, but I guess they have forgotten to tell the Germans. Honestly, the Germans are just plain crazy to keep on fighting. I honestly believe their government, if there is any left, has lost control of the troops. Hell, the Germans don't know what to do or which direction to do it in.

As I told you, the first link up with the Russians has been effected. Now watch for the second one somewhere in the valley of the Danube. From then on, it will be a clean up of the three huge pockets that are left. Boy, the news is good and it has everyone here on edge.

I love you.

Vic (Big)

2 May 45

Hello Sweetheart,

Another liberation picture. Worth is near Landshut and is on the Isar River. One of the boys liberated, Sgt. Peter Taylor, is from Worcester. He is blocked off by me in the picture. Please try to locate his folks and see if they have received word. If not, tell them he is OK.

Everyone here is calling me the Liberator. I like it fine 'cause it sure gives you a good feeling to free these boys. Notice all the boys have guns. They are German guns taken from their prison guards when we jumped them. We liberated about 400 here.

Please notice the German P.W.'s (prisoners of war) standing with their hands over their heads in the background. About 250 of them and still coming in.

Please hold all these snapshots. I'll want them later.

I love you.

Vic (Big)

On the back of this, the only surviving photo is written the following information, unfortunately much of it illegible: "Liberated Americans. American fliers welcome troops of the 13th Armored Division, 3rd U.S. Army after being liberated from German P.O.W. camp near Worth, Germany. These fliers were captured after they were shot down during a raid on Berlin. Left..Lt. Col Rod Francis Jackson of Miss. Shakes hands with Lt. Col. Victor E. Delnore of Worcester, Mass. Task Force Commander CC 13th Armored Division. Other fliers L-R: Lt. Frank K. Jones of Kaysiclle, Utah, Lt. John W. Paul of Balt., Md., Sgt. Herbert V. Evans of Port......., Sgt. Louis Contreras of ...., Sgt. Peter Taylor of Worcester, Mass., Lt. Gerald Zelikovsky of Saratoga Springs, NY, Sgt. Alvin ...rkope of Inez, Texas. ETC HQ 45 34627 29 April. Credit..US Army Signal Corps. Photog..Pvt. T.B. Romero (166)."

Worth, Germany, April 29, 1945: The Liberator

2 May 45
#2

Hello Sweetheart,

Still cold and still raining. I can't figure it. To give you an idea of how cold it has been, here is what I wear starting from the skin out. Cotton undershirt, woolen undershirt, two woolen sweaters, wool shirt, combat jacket, scarf, field jacket and then usually I drape a blanket around my shoulders same as Napoleon. Heck, two months ago I was running around in my shirtsleeves. What a climate. It seems to work in reverse. For the first time since I've been in Europe, I've actually seen it snow. Happened yesterday. I give up.

Well, with Adolf dead*, the war is just about over except for the mopping up. I think the folks back home can start their celebrating. There may be more fighting in the Austrian Alps, but that is all.

I love you.

Vic (Big)

*Adolf Hitler committed suicide on April 30, 1945.

3 May 45
#3

Hello Mommy,

Berlin has fallen and that is good news, but the best news today is the news that the Daddy got from home. Received letters you wrote 12, 14, and 16 April. Also, got a package (at last) from you. Package had candy, nuts, alka seltzer, and two spools of thread. Best of all, it had some funny papers. You should see the boys grab the funnies.

Your letters, as well as the folks', dwelt at great length on President Roosevelt's death. Here we received very little news of it. No details at all. We get very little news at all nowadays. In any event, the boys know it is a great loss to the nation, but everyone is too busy, and I mean busy, to spend much time thinking of it.

Weather is still damned cold, and snow has turned to rain.

I love you.

Vic (Big)

4 May 45
#4

Hello Sweetheart,

From the folks' letters I hear that my little son has really fallen in love with his mother, and that when you leave him he searches all over the house for his Mommy. I also hear that when you are gone, he is not himself again until you return. Well, I think the Daddee (little) is at last really showing real intelligence by appreciating his Mommy same as the Daddy (Big).

It really makes me feel swell to see you and my shadow getting along so well with one another and with everyone else. The folks praise you both to the skies. I want to thank the Mommy for being so nice to my folks. They really appreciate it.

I love you.

Vic (Big)

CHAPTER *IV*

VICTORY AND OCCUPATION

"The Liberator"

On May 1st, Task Force Delnore moved further south to Simbach, and the next day crossed the Inn River into Braunau, Austria, the birthplace of Adolf Hitler. Again the men of the 46th Tank Battalion willingly took on the satisfying task of taking German prisoners and liberating Allied PW's. Captain Kenneth Weaver, commander of Company B, drove behind enemy lines and negotiated with German authorities for the surrender of an entire PW camp located southwest of Braunau, thus liberating 15,000 Allied prisoners, including 4,200 Americans.

Although the routine of occupation and liberation was by now familiar, Braunau did hold one incredible surprise for my father. Among the thousands of Allied prisoners, he found T/Sgt. William Ghiz, a boyhood friend from Worcester, who had been captured by the Germans in 1943. My father's triumphant reunion with his old friend, whom he personally cared for during the next several days, was one of the few war experiences he ever talked about.

By this point, the end of the war in Europe was certain. No sooner would the Americans enter a town than the white flags would appear in the windows, quickly followed by Germans entering the streets with their hands held over their heads. Often so many Germans surrendered at one time that the biggest problem was crowd control.

Beginning in early May, my father's letters reflected a dramatic change, both in tone and in content. Knowledge that victory was not only inevitable but imminent, pride in the fact that his men called him "the Liberator," exhilaration over his reunion with Bill Ghiz, and his newly acquired freedom of expression with the lifting of military censorship — all inspired and made possible letters that were more detailed, more confident, and simply more truthful. His May 22 letter is noteworthy because it began with the announcement that "Now that most of the censorship is off, I can at last reveal our location [Braunau]." From that point on, every letter was headed with the date and the precise location.

Understandably, my father could not resist bragging about his recently earned Bronze Star, Purple Heart, Silver Star, points, and other statistics, including a count of at least 42,000 Allied prisoners of war liberated by the 46th Tank Battalion. He even wrote a personal account of the daring mission at Mudlinghoven, and a few days later sent my mother a copy of the lengthy citation for the Silver Star. Both these letters were typed (a clear indication of more peaceful times) and addressed to his baby son, Victor, Jr. On a more domestic note, my father wrote confidently to my mother of his impending return to his family in America, an expectation punctuated with an urgent plea to my mother to have a medical checkup "now, Sweetheart, 'cause company for Ah-Goo means a lot to me."

My father wrote on the back of this photo: "Austria, at war's end, May 1945."

From early May, when the war in Europe ended, until late June, the 46th Tank Battalion remained in the Braunau-Simbach area, mostly performing the duties of military police. Although strict military regulations forbade fraternization with any Germans, the Americans managed to do some extensive sightseeing. During this period, my father enjoyed several excursions, mostly in Bavaria, which he described as "so beautiful that he could write volumes about it, but they wouldn't tell you half of it."

The third week of June was marked by preparations for the train journey back to France and then on to the U.S.A. The main occupation at this time was packing and getting ready for what my father predicted would be a very uncomfortable trip, since everyone would have to ride in boxcars. Although he "dread[ed] the thought of the train ride," he declared that "we can take anything as long as we are headed in the right direction." By this time, he was "beginning to count the days 'till I see my Mommy again."

5 May 45
Somewhere in Austria

Hello Mommy,

Notice the dateline. Austria. Been here almost a week now. The Daddy didn't want to worry the Mommy about being in combat, but now that the war is over in Europe, he will tell all.

First, let me tell you about our last operation. You read in the papers and heard on the radio that the 13th had captured Hitler's birthplace. Well, the Daddy will take part of the bows. Mine and Smith's* outfit (67) captured the place, and here is the big surprise. About 4 miles away we found 15,000 Allied prisoners of war. 4200 of these were American Air Corps enlisted personnel. That is about the bulk that the Germans held. Well, I looked for and found Willie Ghiz, Eddie's brother. He's OK and in good shape. Please call up his mom and tell her. Also that I'm keeping him with me for a few days.

I love you.

Vic (Big)

*Lt. Col. Ridgeway Smith, commander of the 67th Armored Infantry Battalion

T/Sgt William Ghiz and my father: old friends reunited in Braunau, Austria

6 May 45
#6, Somewhere in Austria

Hello Sweetheart,

Still have Bill Ghiz with me. He put on about two pounds within the past 24 hours. Mommy, our outfit has been in combat about 2 months now. The Daddy has been fighting a bit longer.

So far the Daddy has two decorations. One given to him by the Germans (Purple Heart) for bouncing a bullet off my right shoulder. Everyone in the division makes a joke of it and says my hide is too tough to penetrate. Anyhow, the wound was trifling and didn't even put me out of the fight. The other decoration, I believe, is the Bronze Star, given me for busting thru the

German lines for about three miles with a small group of men, and, believe it or not, we captured 2 Major Generals, 4 full Colonels, 40 other officers, and 650 men. Don't tell anyone, but they were ready to surrender anyway*.

I love you.

Vic (Big)

*The reference here is to the April 17 reconnaissance mission in Mudlinghoven. As he will report in his May 18 letter to his baby son, he was actually awarded the Silver Star for gallantry in action.

Men of the 46th Tank Battalion receiving battle awards from Brig. Gen. Wayland Augur. My father is standing at extreme left.

7 May 45
#7

Hello Sweetheart,

Still cloudy and raining. Not as cold though. Found out the reason yesterday. It cleared for about half an hour, and lo and behold off to the south we could see nothing other than the magnificent, and I mean magnificent, Alps. They make our mountains look like gentle slopes. Stick right up in the air like a finger and are all covered over with snow. When the wind comes from their direction — Brrr.

Willie Ghiz is still with me. First day I got him we gave him a steaming hot bath, haircut, and brand new clothing. After this we fed him a big venison steak with home fries, beans, and coffee. Also white bread. All this was followed by three fried eggs. We then put him to bed in the softest, biggest, and best bed in town. Poor kid, his stomach wasn't used to so much food, and he lost part of the meal during the night.

I love you.

Vic (Big)

7 May 45
Somewhere in Austria

Hello Folks*,

For my money the war is over. I don't care whether it is proclaimed or not. It's all over in Europe. Now that it is over, your son will confess all.

Our outfit has been in action for some time. First we were in the Third Army drive through the Kassel-Erfurt area. We were then moved into the First Army area for the Battle of the Ruhr. We were, upon completion of that

---

*Of all the letters that my father wrote to his parents, this is the only one that has survived. My father's younger brother, Charles Abdelnour, gave it to me to include in this collection.

battle, forced marched back to the Third Army, where we then spearheaded the 3rd Army drive down the Danube valley. My battalion outfit and one other battalion captured Hitler's birthplace, and found Willie Ghiz, who had been a prisoner for exactly 18 months to the day we liberated him. For more details read Catherine's letters.

The soldier boy of the family has been decorated twice. Once with the Purple Heart by the Krauts. Bullet bounced off my shoulder. Skin too thick, couldn't penetrate. The other decoration, the Bronze Star for bravery. See Kitty**, she has more details.

I love you all.

Victor

*my mother's nickname

8 May 45
#8

Hello Mommy,

The war ends officially at 090001. In case you've been away from the Army too long and can't decipher 090001, it means one minute after midnight on the 9th. I guess everyone in the States will celebrate. Here no one is in the mood for a celebration. Too fatigued. However, it sure is wonderful to have the blasted war over with, in Europe anyway.

All three of your packages arrived in good shape yesterday. That makes four I've received. The pictures are wonderful, and I certainly intend keeping them. That kid sure is photogenic. Thanks a million. I'll use everything.

John Arraje (downstairs in our house) called on me yesterday. He is in an outfit that has been attached to the division for a couple of weeks. Been moving too fast and he couldn't catch me. He, Bill Ghiz, and I had quite a reunion. Tell his mom he looks real good. Bill Ghiz is leaving today by plane.

I love you.

Vic (Big)

9 May 45
#9, Still in Austria

Hello Sweetheart,

Got some Syrian music on our radio last night, so I put on a dance for the boys. Three ring circus. V-E Day was no different than any other day here. Germans knew nothing of it and at first refused to believe it when we told them. When at last convinced, they invariably burst into tears.

We are all taking things easy now and getting fat again. The Daddy lost considerable weight. 34 pants hang on me. Last pair bought in U.S. were 38.

We did some figuring last night, and we estimate that our one little battalion liberated at least 42,000 Allied prisoners of war during our drive across Germany. About 12,000 of these were American. Reason we liberated so many was that we usually were the spearhead.

We've lost some of our boys, though nowhere near as many as the other battalions. Of my officers, Jake (Jacobsen) was killed*. Tattkop and Jackson** pretty badly wounded. Moore*** was captured, but we recaptured him 10 days later. Others were slightly wounded.

Love,
Vic (Big)

*Captain Harold Jacobsen was killed in combat in Hassels, Germany in mid-April of 1945.

**On April 15, 1945, Captain George Jackson was seriously wounded by the same German bullet that wounded General Wogan in the throat and my father in the shoulder.

***First Lieutenant Fred Moore was in Company A of the 46th Tank Battalion.

10 May 45
#10

Dear Sweetheart,

Well, the weather has taken a sudden turn for the better. Woke yesterday to find blazing sunshine, birds twittering, flies all over the place, etc., and all this change occurred within a twenty-four hour period. Today the weather is just perfect. I'm going out and take a sunbath.

The Daddy is now the proud owner of a portable victrola, purchased for 100 francs. So I need phonograph needles (best type), and how about some records. Celluloid type records are best. You know the type of tunes the Daddy likes best. We need the records pronto as it is our only source of dance music for our Battalion Officers Club. Show this letter to the postal authorities.

By the time you receive this letter, it ought to be pretty close to your birthday. As usual, I can't send you anything but greetings, but, honey, I want you to know I love you very much, would rather be with you than with anyone else in the world. Happy Birthday.

Vic (Big)

[The next document is a prewritten Mother's Day Card, almost as cliché ridden as the Easter card from a few weeks before. The card is signed in ink "The Daddy."]

On this, Your Day, of all the days,
Throughout the passing year,
I send my love and gratitude
To one I hold most dear
And may my wish for happiness
In everything you do
Be Yours this day and every day
Until our dreams come true.

11 May 45
#11

Good Morning Sweetheart,

Now that we are back on a garrison basis, first thing I do is say "Good Morning" to the Mommy and the Daddee, whose large pictures sit on the Daddy's huge and beautiful desk. Right after I say "Good Morning," I write you your daily letter.

We are back in shirtsleeves again. Today gives promise of being even more beautiful than yesterday. My headquarters has taken over the courthouse of a fairly large town. Beautiful building. I have taken the Judge's office for my office. It's a piperoo. Makes me feel awfully important.

My window flies the only American flag within 50 miles. Honestly, the presence of that flag makes me feel wonderful. In all our battles, as soon as we took a town, sometimes even while the shooting was going on, we'd hoist our flag. Once up the gang never gave an inch.

I love you.

Vic (Big)

12 May 45
#12

Good Morning Sweetheart,

Another beautiful day. Today I'm going to tell you about DP (Displaced Personnel). In Germany there was no poor class. The suckers who did the menial labor were the different nationalities brought in, chiefly French, Russian, Pole. These people were farmed out to farms and factories. The factory group live in small shacks.

As we overran Germany, these people were liberated. We'd no sooner hit town than most of them would start looting and reaping vengeance on the

Germans. Much as we sympathize with them, we were forced to stop them. The deeper we got into Germany, the greater the problem of controlling these people was. If a town was well garrisoned with German soldiers who were able to control these people until we overcame the resistance, things weren't so bad.

Continue tomorrow.

I love you.

Vic (Big)

13 May 45
#13

Good Morning Sweetheart,

Vicki's birthday today. Adele's* 15th. Pop's 17th. Undy's 21st. Yours 26th. Margie's** was 11th. What a month. Happy Birthday to all.

To continue with my story...However, if the German garrison had pulled out, the German people would be in a tough spot. Often they would remove all road blocks, disarm all German soldiers remaining in town, cut the wire on any demolitions planted in bridges, and send a delegation out to meet us with a Red Cross flag. They'd beg us to stay in their town, offering inducements such as best houses to live in, liquor, girls, etc.

If we intended to stay and we wanted to boost the price up, all we had to do was be sorry but the Russians are supposed to take over this area. They are right behind us. We must move on. Honestly, they'd go frantic and plead with us to stay. If of necessity we had to go, the population would line the streets and just bawl their eyes out. Serves the bastards right.

I love you.

Vic (Big)

*my father's first cousin, Adele Abdelnour
**my father's sister-in-law, Margie Abdelnour, married to his brother Eddie

14 May 45

Good morning, Sweetheart,

Starting our 5th month of separation today, but with the victory over Germany we are that much closer to being together again.

To get back to the DP's...For the past two months the roads have been jammed with these people all trying to get home. About two days after a town is taken and all PW's rounded up, we round up all displaced personnel and send them on their way home or to camps, where they are housed and fed. They are a terrific problem. So many of them.

Honestly, Germany had everyone working for her. I am trying to give you a picture of this, but I just know I am not doing a good job. Hell, there probably will be a good article about it in one of the magazines. The point is the Dutch, Germans, Russians, French, Poles, Czechs, Hungarians, Danes, Belgians, and all the others are on their way home. Everyone you see is going home, that is, all except the Americans.

I love you.

Vic (Big)

15 May 45
#15

Good morning, Sweetheart,

Another beautiful day. We've been having perfect weather since 4 May. It seems that as soon as we stopped fighting, the weather, which had been nasty for three weeks, turned perfect. I guess it's nature's way of showing approval.

We have been sitting in the same place for two weeks now doing very little. Got a mission to chase down some of these hair-brained werewolves or die-hard SS troops. They are nowhere near as tough as they are cracked up to be. Scare themselves more than anyone else.

Yesterday we captured the German Ambassador to Hungary. He was hiding out in a small village nearby. His own people squealed on him. Funny thing about these Germans, they squeal on one another and think absolutely nothing of it. Of course, my announcing that any house sheltering one of these birds would be burned to the ground — with a practical demonstration — may have had something to do with it.

Ah-Goo's and your picture is sure nice to look at. I love you.

Vic (Big)

Another photo of my mother and brother, which my father kept with him while he was in Europe

16 May 45
#16

Good morning, Honey,

Weather is even nicer today. Really makes you enjoy life. Received four letters from you yesterday. Also received the *Knights Journal*. Story on Bill Ghiz is a bit off, but it sure made good reading*.

Glad to hear that my little man is getting along so well in his speech. Only hope he doesn't argue too much with me later.

Henry Ebert was telling the boys yesterday about how I got drunk on Victor's birthday, and how I brought all those officers in to see the both of you way after visiting hours. I sure was a proud man on that day and no fooling. I just remembered. Put the doctor's bill on Ah-Goo's ear in the book. I'm building up my case against him now. I'll need the head start from the looks of things.

I love you both.

Vic (Big)

*The local newsletter confused the early May liberation of the PW camp at Braunau, Austria, where my father found Bill Ghiz, with the April 29 liberation of the PW camp at Worth, Germany.

17 May 45
#17

Good morning to the Mommy and to the Daddee,

It sure is nice to have your pictures on the desk in front of me. That one of Ah Goo is a pippin. 'Course the one of the Mommy is nice too, but then the Mommy always looked good to the Daddy.

Glad to hear that you received the Nazi flag*. That flag was presented to the town of Schonenburg (just east of Zweibrucken) by Adolf. Your Daddy's

*Soon after my father's death in 1998, my mother found the Nazi flag, a gift from Adolf Hitler to the town of Schonenburg, in a basement trunk. She donated it to the Boylston Historical Society, along with a letter explaining its significance. Incidentally, an article in the *Worcester Daily Telegram*, dated June 15, 1945, erroneously reported that the flag had been a gift from Hitler to the town of Braunau.

gang captured it last April. We had the American flag flying from the City Hall of that town within five minutes after we entered it. Boy, was that gang of Heinies scared of us.

There are some other souvenirs on the way, chiefly machine guns. The Daddy didn't have much time for souvenirs 'cause we seldom stopped. It's the gang that follows behind that gets all the stuff. Me, I'd rather be up front fighting the Krauts than in rear robbing them.

I love you.

Vic (Big)

18 May 45
#18, Austria

Good morning, Sweetheart,

Weather is getting better day by day now. It's really beautiful. This place has Blue Ridge Summit or anything else I've seen in the U.S. topped a mile. Remember how I used to rave to you about the French countryside? Well, multiply that by ten and you have Germany and Austria. Any spot in these two countries is more beautiful and better laid out than Green Hill Park*. No fooling. Our boys just look and gasp.

I hope the good old U.S. looks like this during my lifetime. There are no billboards, signs, hot dog stands, or shacks of any kind along the roads. That sure makes a big difference. Cities aren't as nice as the U.S., but they sure are clean. The people are responsible for the sidewalks and street in front of their homes, and they actually scrub them daily.

I love you.

Vic (Big)

*Another reference to the public park in Worcester, Massachusetts, that seems to have been my father's standard for natural beauty.

18 May 45

Hello Daddee,

Thought you might be interested to know that instead of getting the Bronze Star, I have received the Silver Star, which is a higher award. Needless to say, I am very happy and proud to receive the decoration and thought, seeing as how you are me, you might like to know about it too so you could do a little bragging to your Mommy. Here is how the citation reads:

By direction of the President, under the provisions of AR 600-45, 22 September 1943, as amended, the Silver Star is awarded to VICTOR E. DELNORE, 0 337 481, Lieutenant Colonel, Infantry, Headquarters 46th Tank Battalion, for gallantry in action on 17 April 1945 in the vicinity of Mudlinghoven, Germany.

Apprised of a possible enemy headquarters for anti-aircraft units, Lieutenant Colonel Delnore organized a volunteer commando task force from his Reconnaissance Platoon and advanced rapidly across open terrain. He evaded German 88mm fire from the woods to the east by heading toward a draw northwest of hostile guns. Encountering small arms fire, Lieutenant Colonel Delnore regrouped his men, minus supporting troops, and made a run for the enemy Command Post. The element of surprise was so great that the surrender of two Major Generals, their staffs, and 600 enemy flak troops was effected without a single American casualty. This officer's bravery, skill and exceptional devotion to duty reflect high credit upon himself and the Army. Entered military service from Worcester, Massachusetts.

I hope you are a little bit proud of your Daddy. A longer narrative account, which goes into much more detail, is attached to the citation, but as yet I haven't received it. When I do I will send it on to you. Included in the capture were four full colonels and at least fifty other officers. Don't tell your Mommy, but there were two WACS there too, but that is another story.

Bye, Daddee. Kiss Mommy for me.

Daddy

19 May 45
#19

Good morning Sweetheart,

At last that award has come thru and with what a surprise. Instead of getting the Bronze Star, I got the Silver Star, a much higher decoration. Less than 6 have been given out in the division to date. Reason for the higher award was that the capture we made just about folded up the Ruhr pocket and was directly responsible for the surrender of Dusseldorf.

I was in Dusseldorf the evening of 17 April for about four hours. Two days later you can imagine my consternation when, on the evening of the 19th, while sitting on the outskirts of the town, we heard a broadcast which stated that the Ruhr battle was over with the exception of Dusseldorf, which was resisting fiercely. All the boys went out and took a look, but we could see there had been no shooting for two days. Made us feel awful funny to hear it though.

Has Bill Ghiz reached home yet?

My task force was 11 men.

I love you.

Vic (Big)

20 May 45
#20

Good morning, Sweetheart,

I suppose this point system has everyone at home excited. To set your mind at rest, I'll tell you how I stand. My points are figured:

Length of Service w/overseas	60	(56 mos. 4 overseas)
Awards, Battle Stars	15	(Battle of Germany Purple Heart Silver Star)

Dependent children	12
	———
	87

So you see, if I were an enlisted man, I would stand a pretty good chance of getting out, but being an officer, the same system does not hold. My ratings of Superior kill about any chance I would have of getting out. Besides, I don't want to. War is not over yet.

I probably shouldn't tell you, but here goes. I have asked to be retained in the service until the emergency is over. I don't feel that I'm not being fair to you and Victor. On the contrary, I feel that this is the only way you both would have it. I hope I'm right.

I love you.

Vic (Big)

⇒⟨⇐

21 May 45
#21

Good morning, Mommy,

I missed my family very much day before yesterday. You see, I went on a sightseeing trip to Salzburg-Berchtesgaden-Giminder See-Possau-Ried, and then back home. It was the first such trip in seven years in which I didn't have my sweetheart by my side. I did the best I could with make believe, but I am afraid I wasn't very convincing. The trip was very worthwhile. Scenery is beyond words. Hitler's home was a complete wreck — compliments of the Air Corps.

Things are really dull here. After the excitement of war, peace, though wonderful, is dull, mainly because we have little or no social life. We are not permitted to even speak to the Germans. Pretty rough on the boys 'cause some of the Austrian (Germans to us) gals are really a knockout, and they really throw their eyes at the boys. No American gals within 50 miles.

I love you.

Vic

22 May 45

Hello, Daddee,

Here is that narrative part of the citation.

At approximately 1530, 17 April 1945, a message was received at the Command Post of the 46th Battalion directing that Task Force Delnore, under the command of Lt. Col. Victor E. Delnore, 0337481, to attack [sic] immediately for Mudlinghoven, Germany (F425918), approximately three miles north of Erkrath, Germany, the position of Task Force Delnore at that time. Their mission was to advance to Mudlinghoven and seize the enemy headquarters believed to be the Command Post of all flak troops in that area. Lt. Col. Delnore responded to the order with enthusiasm.

Believing that a compact, volunteer force, organized as a commando unit could better accomplish the mission than an unwieldy force of tanks and infantry, Lt. Col. Delnore called for volunteers from his Reconnaissance platoon, Headquarters Company, 46th Task Battalion. A task force of five reconnaissance 1/4 ton trucks was organized under the personal command of Lt. Col. Delnore. Having explained the mission to the Task Force, Lt. Col. Delnore led the unit northwest out of Erkrath.

Advancing rapidly across open terrain north of the railroad, vicinity (F410930), the party encountered enemy 88mm flak fire from the woods to the east. Directing the following vehicles to increase speed, Lt. Col. Delnore evaded this enemy fire by cutting towards a draw northwest of the 88mm position. Regrouping, the task force again cut across the field to the northeast. As they approached the woods in that vicinity, the party received small arms fire. Signaling the attacking party to continue with the advance, Lt. Col. Delnore speeded into defilade cover prior to continuing to the north. Again regrouping his force, and with no supporting troops at hand, Lt. Col. Delnore decided to make a run for the enemy command post.

Advancing upon Mudlinghoven as a flying squad, Lt. Col. Delnore saw an enemy officer in uniform at the window of a house situated at the top of the hill on the outskirts of the town. Signaling the party to stop and to surround the premises, Lt. Col. Delnore ran into the house. The speed of the attack obviated any resistance from enemy security detachments, and so surprised the enemy officers in the command post that surrender was given immediately.

Lt. Col. Delnore, by his daring and courageous action in leading the task force, accomplished the surrender through the enemy officers of all enemy flak troops in that area, totaling approximately six hundred troops, including two Major Generals. The entire operation was conducted without casualty to our forces.

Daddee, we started with 5 jeeps, but the enemy fire was too heavy. We got there with only three. The other two came up 10 minutes later. The first three jeeps counting mine had 11 men besides your Daddy. OK?

Your Daddy

22 May 45
#22, Braunau, Austria

Good morning, Sweetheart,

Now that most of the censorship is off, I at last can reveal our location. Happy now?

Before I left home, I told Ah-Goo to check up on you. That's why he was awake when you came in at 4 a.m. I received letters dated 6, 7, 9, and 11 May. Last letter had the clipping. Too bad Sgt. Taylor couldn't have been in the picture so his mother could be certain it was he. You may have found me out, but you didn't do so until the war was over, which was what I wanted 'cause I didn't want the Mommy worrying.

Nice of Ruthie* to call you. Here's some news for you. Same bullet that hit Wogan, then hit me, and then hit Jackson. Jackson almost died. Had to give him four blood transfusions. Wogan was pretty bad for a while, but I kept him in the hole and took care of him, then got him to a doctor (more on that later). See why they call the Daddy tough? They bounce off.

My name has gone in for another decoration. 92 points.

I love you.

Vic (Big)

*Ruthie was Capt. Henry Ebert's wife. The Eberts and the Delnores had been friends since their days in Brownwood, Texas.

23 May 45
#23, Braunau, Austria

Good morning, Sweetheart,

Weather still is something to talk about. Perfect. Mommy, you keep giving me the devil for not having given you more dope as to what went on. I couldn't and I didn't, nor did anyone else I know of pass on info to their folks back home. Most of them got their dope from reading the papers.

New York papers were full of the movements and doings of our division for a long time. I am amazed that you did not run across any of them. Nearly all the large papers in the country covered us. Hit the headlines more than once. They were calling us " Patton's Phantom Armored Division" 'cause we were moving so fast no one, not even the people directly over us, and sometimes not even we ourselves, knew where we were. Many a time my little outfit would be ten miles in the German lines all by itself. Absolutely no one around to help us. Best solution was to keep going and keep Germans off balance. It worked.

I love you.

Vic (Big)

24 May 45
#24, Braunau, Austria

Good morning, Sweetheart,

Drizzling rain today. A bit of a relief. Just about all censorship is off. 'Bout the only thing I can't write about is future movements, so you can ask me about any questions you want now and I'll answer them for you.

In case you are interested, we landed at Le Havre, France on the 29th of January. We put into port at Southampton, England on the 28th, but did not disembark. Had quite a lot of trouble the last three days with submarines. Our ship was one of the few ships that had no girls on board. Damn! Made up for it since, however.

From Le Havre we went to Beaunay, which you know all about already. People were really wonderful to us there. I wish you would read the papers thoroughly. During the last month of the war, we drew more space than any other division, mainly because we were in the lead.

Love,
Vic (Big)

25 May 45
#25

Good morning, Mommy,

Heard from Henry that you visited Ruth. Ruth says you've recovered your figure and really look lovely. That's for me. Hope Mommy stays that way.

Your people keep asking me for requests for packages. OK. How about a box of Fanny Farmer's every two weeks? Sure miss having candy. No, I'm not pregnant! You can supplement that with Hershey bars or other nickel bars. How about those records? Now am I selfish enough to suit you?

I've sent you some Nazi dress bayonets. They're to be given as souvenirs to both our families or friends as you wish. Please try to find out what the others want and I'll try to get them. I haven't had much time for souvenir hunting. Never cared much about them anyway.

I love you.

Vic (Big)

26 May 45
#26, Braunau, Austria

Happy Birthday to the Mommy*.

I wish you the happiest birthday that anyone ever had, and I pray that you spend all your other birthdays in my company.

Just think, Mommy, the first of your birthdays that you and I celebrated together was your 18th. I well remember how dumbfounded I was to find out that it was only your 18th. Heck, I had taken you to be at least three years older. Although you didn't come right out and lie about your age, you sure didn't do anything about correcting the false impression that I had, you little minx. All is forgiven now on account of the Ah-Goo anyway.

I want the Mommy to know that she looks lovelier now than she did when I married her. You looked the prettiest on our trip to New York.

All kinds of love.

Vic (Big)

*May 26, 1945 was my mother's 25th birthday.

27 May 45
#27, Braunau, Austria

Good morning, Sweetheart,

Another beautiful Sunday. Been here too long already and we are all getting a little bit restless. After work hours there is absolutely nothing to do. In France we could go chasing mademoiselles or visiting French families, but here no soap. This no fraternization thing is really tough. We are not even permitted to go into a store to buy anything. Never speak to a civilian. Just Army-Army all the time.

Everyone is hoping and praying that they move us back to France and quick. About the only recreation we have is hunting, sightseeing, movies twice a week, and weekend softball games. No cafes, no music, no nurses, no nothing.

Got that off my chest. I'm better off than most 'cause I have my Mommy and Daddee to think and dream about.

I love you.

Vic (Big)

28 May 45
#28, Braunau, Austria

Good morning, Sweetheart,

Been thinking a lot about you and little Victor today. I still remember him coming to me just before I left to go to New York. He rubbed his eyes and laid his head against my knee. When I asked him, "Sleepy, daddee?" he raised his arms for me to pick him up. I put him to bed and played with him for a minute. He responded as usual by laughing his head off. Time 1235, 14 Jan. 45.

Does he still behave as well when you put him to bed? How about that laugh? Does he still play radio-operator? What about that ticket-toi business? Tell me how else he has changed. You have been pretty good about telling me of his new tricks, but what about the old? How are his dancing lessons coming along?

I hope the Mommy has sent those phonograph records. I'm tired of listening to the German pieces I got with the phonograph.

I love you both very much.

Vic (Big)

Two of the many V-mails that my father wrote: On April 18, he commented that he had yet to run into anyone from the hill, his old Worcester neighborhood. Less than three weeks later, he happily recounted his reunion in Austria with just such a person, his childhood friend, Bill Ghiz, who had been a POW for 18 months.

29 May 45
#29, Braunau, Austria

Good morning, Mommy,

Thanks a million for permission to be a bad boy, but I'll have to take a rain check on it. Reason: I am not permitted to have dealings with Germans, displaced personnel are not worthy of the Mommy, no WACs or nurses anywhere near us. Thanks anyway, pal.

Your letter of the 19th reached here yesterday. Last preceding letter was 14th. Hope others get here today.

Mommy, you ask about the Pacific. My own idea is that just about everyone is going to the Pacific sooner or later. I know nothing definite. Promise to keep you posted just as soon as I find out anything, that is, if I am permitted to divulge the information. You know me. As for coming home for a leave, I know nothing. I hesitate to build up or to dash your hopes. Hence I haven't said anything. Really, honey, anything I say is a wild guess.

I love you.

Vic (Big)

30 May 45
#30, Braunau, Austria

Good morning, Sweetheart,

It is now 0730. That is the time I usually write your letter. See, Mommy, first thoughts every day are of you and Victor.

Received a long letter from Pete. He sounds pretty disheartened. I guess it's that way aboard ship. I'll answer him soon.

Mail lately has been poor. Hope I get some today. Life is pleasant, but oh how dull. Wish they'd move us back to France, where I can parlay with the mademoiselles. I'm losing my touch because of lack of practice.

Have the little toy automobiles I sent Victor arrived yet? They are really good. At least one of them can be halted merely by shouting at it.

Gosh but the Mommy's picture sure is beautiful. How about another 5 x8 of just your head?

I love you both.

Vic (Big)

31 May 45
#31, Braunau, Austria

Good morning, Mommy,

Pouring rain today. Received your 2 page letter dated 21 May. Your letters have not been coming in in the same order you mailed them. I hadn't even known you'd gone on the trip. Glad you had a good time and happy to know you liked Mrs. Ebert. Seems like she has some sense. Too bad she can't pass on some of that common sense to Ruthie. She needs it. Henry is no different from any other man.

So the Mommy was able to resist temptation, huh? Not for the Daddy, mind you, but because of the Baby. Well, I'll confess something too. He has come between me and more than one mademoiselle, if you get what I mean.

No news at all of any anticipated moves. Henry is nuts telling his mother about coming home 'cause how can he know? Just think of the disappointment if he's wrong.

I love you.

Vic (Big)

1 June 45
#1, Braunau, Austria

Good morning, Sweetheart,

Received your letter of 22 May yesterday. Sweetheart, I can't understand why my mail hasn't reached you, as I have written you every day to date. Honestly. Your mail too is coming in in dribbles. So far I have received the following letters this month: 2nd, 3rd, 5th, 6th, 7th, 9th, 10th, 11th, 13th, 14th, 19th, 21st, and 22nd. Big gap between 14th and 19th.

I think I have written more this month (May) than any other inasmuch as two of the letters entirely separate from yours, were addressed to Victor. In addition, my mail to my folks was stepped up around the 10th.

I do hope that the mail gets in to you and soon. It is still pouring rain out. No new information, but the rumors are fast and furious. Will let you know as much as I can when there is something more definite.

Glad to hear Victor is an accomplished orator.

I love you.

Vic (Big)

2 June 45
#2, Braunau, Austria

Good morning, Sweetheart,

Rumors are sure traveling fast in this outfit. Never saw anything like it. Don't pay any attention to them myself. However, here is my guess as to what happens to us.

We won't be used as occupational troops. We will go to the Pacific*. When we go, I bet 10 to 1 it's by way of the U.S. and that we will be there at least three months.

---

*The 46th Tank battalion was selected for the anticipated attack on Tokyo Bay.

I don't like to guess on anything like this, but the Mommy has been so demanding, I feel that I have to say something. I hope that we are not disappointed.

Seeing as how I may come home, you'd better have the doctor check you over right away. It means a lot to me, honey. That little shadow of mine is going to have someone to grow up with if I can help it.

I love you.

Vic (Big)

3 June 45
#3, Braunau, Austria

Good morning, Mommy,

Another beautiful Sunday. It is now 1110. Going to church at 1130. Having General Auger for dinner at 1230. After that I think I'll go out and take a sunbath. Life is rough in the ETO*.

Mommy, I wrote you sometime ago and asked you to see what you, Naj, Vicki, and Charlie could do to get the folks to move off the hill. So far I have received no word from you, Chick, or Naj on the subject. Let me know how you are doing.

I hope the Mommy takes my message to visit a doctor for a checkup seriously. I never meant anything more in my life. Please do it now, Sweetheart, 'cause company for Ah-Goo means a lot to me.

I love you all very much.

Vic (Big)

*European Theater of Operation

4 June 45
#4, Braunau, Austria

Good morning, Mommy,

Another beautiful day. Never too warm and never too cool nowadays. Ideal. Spent all afternoon yesterday sunbathing. Everyone here does it.

These Kraut girls around here sure make the boys' temperatures rise when they go sunbathing, which is about every day. Girls here in Germany dress like and look like the girls back home, except that they don't paint their faces up as much. They are not as modest as you all are and think nothing about exposing, and I mean exposing, their legs. They wear slacks, shorts, skimpy dresses, etc.

Most of the girls are well built due to the gymnastic exercises they have been put through. There is one big trouble with them, though. They nearly all look like horses. No fooling. I'll take the Mommy.

Vic (Big)

5 June 45
#5, Simbach, Germany

Good morning, Mommy,

Moved across the river into Germany. Simbach and Braunau are twin cities just across the Inn River from each other. Of the two cities I like Simbach better. They still haven't moved any American girls yet, and things are getting real tough. About all we can do is keep the boys real busy.

The German civilians have gotten over being scared of us and are beginning to make demands. We're not allowed to sit on them as we used to during wartime because military government has moved in and they are pretty chicken hearted with them. The Germans know better than to get uppity with our battalion 'cause we had to fight to take this area, and we had some of our boys hurt. We just remind them of that and the conversation comes to an abrupt end.

I love you.

Vic (Big)

6 June 45
#6, Simbach, Germany

Good morning, Sweetheart,

Today is a holiday for us. Anniversary for D Day. Received letters dated 26, 27, 28 May. So far letters for 1st, 4th, 8th, 12th, 15th, 16th, 20th, 22nd are missing, that is, if you wrote on those days. I haven't missed, so you can expect a letter for each day.

The phonograph records are a gift from you to me. I hope you consulted Najla on the type records I wanted. Records with vocals of any length are no good. I want dance records with a bumpy rhythm. Remember how the Daddy liked to dance to them.

I caught the grippe 'cause I was run down. 12 days and nights without sleep. We had a five day break, so I went to bed for four of them. German women took care of me.

Sure looks like my shadow is getting to be quite a speaker. Guess the Mommy really loves him. Save some of that love for me.

Guess I'll take a sunbath today.

I love you.

Vic (Big)

7 June 45
#7, Simbach, Germany

Good morning, Sweetheart,

Weather still perfect.

A mark is worth 10 cents in American money on the exchange. However, in actual purchase value it's worth 35 to 40 cents. So the victrola cost me $10. Same thing in the States would have cost about $35. The victrola (portable) is a really nice one. Its tone is superior to any made in America that I have heard.

Mommy, you kids ask me what I want. OK. How about a package with some small cans of things like sardines, anchovies, tuna, etc.? I refuse to accept anything that costs points*. So help me, I'll send it back.

Jackson got back from the hospital about four days ago. That bullet sure tore the hell out of his right arm. Scar is six inches long right across the inside of the elbow. Outside of a numb feeling in the arm, it doesn't bother him a bit.

I forgot to tell you but Doc Biddle too came back to us about four weeks ago. Friedman, Laverty, and Nolte transferred.

I love you.

Vic (Big)

---

*Americans at home bought food using a rationing system whereby different items that were in demand were assigned points. When someone purchased one of these items, he or she had points deducted from a monthly allotment, which was kept track of with a ration book. Foods that were not in big demand did not cost points — you could buy as much as you were willing to pay for. In this letter my father is insisting that my mother send him only items that will not cost her points.

8 June 45
#8, Simbach, Germany

Good morning, Sweetheart,

Another beautiful day. Never had such a run of nice weather. The Daddy is turning more and more brown. You probably won't recognize me when you see me. Not too much work. Nice easy life, but I sure do miss the Mommy and the Daddee now that my mind is more free.

We've had an evacuation hospital move in 16 miles away. I think every office for a hundred miles called on them.

The Daddy did all right on account of his dancing. If you want that shadow of mine to be a success with the gals, you'd better see to it that he gets his daily dancing lesson. I hadn't danced in such a long time I thought I'd forgotten how, but no sirree, I still cut a fancy rug. Got the Mommy jealous enough? I'll tell you a secret. No matter with whom I dance I make believe it's you.

Love,
Vic (Big)

9 June 45
#9, Simbach, Germany

Good morning, Sweetheart,

It is certain now, Sweetheart, that you need that medical examination I spoke of in my letters. It will be about the date I told my folks.

Things here are a bit hum drum. Funniest incident of the week occurred to O'Malley. Made a date to visit a Polish girl he had met for the first time at her home. The street address she gave him had a letter and five numbers, as well as the name of the street. He didn't notice this, though, and just stuck the address in his pocket. When he called he couldn't find any houses on the street, which ran parallel to a railroad track. You guessed it. The number given was the number of the boxcar she lived in. It happens here every day.

I love you.

Vic (Big)

10 June 45
#10, Simbach, Germany

Good morning, Sweetheart,

Received your letters 31 May and 1 June. You can give one each of those toy autos to Danny and Everett* if you wish. I'd like to send them some souvenirs, but find it difficult. I was too busy in combat, and nothing is left. If you wish to, you can give them each a Nazi sword. I've sent you six. Probably haven't arrived yet. They are OK for them 'cause they are very short, no point, and no cutting edge. I can get weapons, but they are not allowing them through the mails. Besides, not suitable for them.

Mommy, I hope you are using this opportunity at home to learn how to cook Syrian style. It always was a disappointment to me that you didn't do more of it. I realize that some of the ingredients were hard to get. Please, Mommy, learn how. Baking bread too, huh?

I love you.

Vic (Big)

*young nephews of my mother

11 June 45
#11, Simbach, Germany

Good morning, Mommy,

Dreary cool day today, but not too bad. We're all busy as hell now, getting ready to leave this country for La Belle France. Fraternization country. Hurray! Sheffey and the rest of the boys are really anxious to talk?? to the French girls. Sheffey swears he is going to surround himself with six of them all the time he is in France.

Received the *Knights Journal*. Nice letter from Bill Ghiz. The club is a bit mixed up though. The liberation of the fliers at Worth, whose picture the newspapers ran, was entirely separate from this one on Bill Ghiz, as I explained to you in my letters.

Tell Rachel I love her dearly, and anytime she can get up enough courage, I'll take her out.

Love,
Vic (Big)

12 June 45
#12, Simbach, Germany

Good morning to the Sweetest Mommy in the World,

Sure do spend a lot of time thinking and talking about you and Victor. Can't even begin to tell you how anxious I am to see you again.

Troops are really moving out for the States now. Johnny Arrage's outfit is moving out today. He ought to be home in 6 weeks. Tell his Mommy 'cause he is a poor letter writer. He dropped over to see me Sunday night. He sure has changed for the better.

I'm beginning to be able to speak a little German. It's a pretty tough language, but not as tough to us as English is to the Krauts. I never appreciated how difficult English was until I saw foreigners trying to learn it.

Got a date to take a nurse to a dance. She asked me. She is married too. I love you.

Vic (Big)

13 June 45
#13, Simbach, Germany

Good morning, Sweetheart,

Pouring rain out. Really rough. Sweetheart, please don't mail me any more packages, as I'm pretty sure they won't get to me on time.

Pretty near packed for our move to France, which we should start this Sunday. We are going to an area just south of Rheims.

Had a little party here last night. Some nurses came over. The Daddy is still the best dancer in the division. I think I loved the girl I was paired off with.

Your pictures taken on Palm Sunday had just come in, so I dragged out all the other old pictures I had and insisted on showing them. Can't help bragging about my Mommy and my little Daddee 'cause I love them both so much.

Received a letter from Ruth Ebert. She thinks a lot of you.

Vic (Big)

14 June 45
#14, Simbach, Germany

Good morning, Mommy,

Weather has cleared at last, but it sure is cold. The Daddy has put back most of the weight he lost in combat. Just got back from having a nice piece of steak for breakfast that our cook held out for me since last night.

Received your 31 May letter yesterday. Mail sure comes in funny.

You asked me to tell you something about myself. There is nothing to tell. I look the same, feel better. My wound has never been any trouble except that it itches. Have a fairly hard time keeping busy, but manage to do all right.

Gen. Auger is still with us. He was relieved for a short time during combat, but is now back. Feldman is now a major. Sheffey is the same. Still claims you're the best cook in the world. He's nuts. Your Mommy is. Why the heck don't you learn how to cook Syrian style?

I love you anyway.

Vic (Big)

15 June 45
#15, Simbach, Germany

Good morning, Sweetheart,

Damn! It's raining again today. Cool, too. Went to a dance last night at Pocking (near Passau). Had a heck of a good time, but missed the Mommy something terrible. The Daddy was a social success on account of his dancing. Had a bit of a difficult time, though, 'cause usually I go stag and dance with all the girls. Last night I was asked by a very nice gal from New Orleans, and I had to stick fairly close to her, which I didn't mind in the least. However, some of the girls did, and, whether you believe it or not, I was asked by five different ones (and not bad, too) to dance with them.

For a fat, old, baldheaded man, that is not so bad. So, Mommy, if you want our son to get his pick of the girls, you'd better see to it that he learns to dance and well.

I love the Mommy.

Vic (Big)

16 June 45
#16, Simbach, Germany

Good morning, Sweetheart,

Weather is OK again. Saw a movie last night. Getting so we get movies regularly now. No mail from you for three days. Expect a batch today.

In one of your letters you make reference to two bayonets. The bayonets I meant were purely dress type with one side a saw edge and pointless. I sent you six of these. I'd like for some of our friends to get one of these. I can't get any souvenirs. We aren't permitted to buy anything in the stores. Anyone who does (and there are plenty) is violating the law.

Everyone is expecting the non-fraternization rules against the Austrians to end today. They would now that we are on the German side of the river. Well, I'll swim the doggone thing.

I love you and I miss you very much.

Vic (Big)

17 June 45
#17, Simbach, Germany

Good morning, Sweetheart,

Rained cats and dogs last night, but cleared for today. Had a picnic planned for today, but had to call it off 'cause the nurses we were taking moved this morning. Everybody is moving. Even our outfit should be leaving here by next Sunday.

As I told you, we go to a camp just south of Rheims. Stay there a week, then move off to a port and home. I think you can call it a safe bet that I'll be seeing you by about 1 Aug, and possibly by Ah-Goo's birthday*. Can't tell you how happy I feel about it. I'll have about one month with you, then we

---

*July 20

go back to duty and training for about 2 months in the States. Hope you'll be able to come with me for those two months.

I am trying to arrange it so I can get to Brest to check on Undy.

Love,
Vic

18 June 45
#18, Simbach, Germany

Good morning, Mommy,

Received your letter of 8 June yesterday. Honey, I think our little fellow is rude to Helen* and I'd like for you to correct this. She's too good to him.

Don't worry about my weight. I've put back what I've lost. I'm healthier now than when I left you. I'm a bit on the nervous side, but then that always happened to me when we're separated. I hope you've gotten my summer uniforms out ready for wear. I'm going to need them.

I've been thinking of where we might stay for that month I'm home.

If we weren't going to do any running around, visiting Tooma, etc., I'd be tempted to take an apartment just so I could enjoy the little fellow and you all the more.

Gen. Wogan is at Walter Reed Hospital in Washington**. If you are down that way, stop in to see him.

I love you.

Vic (Big)

*my mother's sister-in-law, Helen Abdelmaseh

**After being seriously wounded on April 15 in Manfort, Germany, Maj. Gen. Wogan was sent back to the United States for medical treatment. His position as 13th Armored Division commander was taken over by Maj. Gen. John Millikin.

19 June 45
#19, Simbach, Germany

Good morning, Sweetheart,

Received your letters dated 5 June and 10 June. Thanks for sending the records so promptly, although I don't expect them to arrive before we leave.

Mommy, don't give my shoulder another thought. Honestly, the wound never bothered me for even a second except for the doggoned itching when it was healing. Forget it!

Ran into Ed Kormanzos. Their second child was a girl, and Ed is real proud to have her. I see from your letters that my little fellow has really changed. I hope not too much 'cause I sure liked him the way he was. Glad to know that you do spank him when he misbehaves. Nothing better for bringing him up right.

Going on a sightseeing trip this afternoon to Cheim See (southeast of Munich).

I love you.

Vic (Big)

20 June 45
#20, Simbach, Germany

Good morning, mommy,

Back from my trip to Cheim See. What a beautiful place. Honestly, honey, you have no idea how beautiful southern Germany is. If the GI's here have their way, there are going to be some changes made in the good old U.S. when we get back.

That bunch of nurses that moved away from us moved to Cheim See and invited me down to see their new place. God! What a place. I haven't seen anything like it before. Makes Tahoe look like a picnic ground. I got there too late to see the place yesterday, so I am going down again tonight to a dance. Stay over and really look the place over tomorrow. I promise to try to be good, but you know me.

Sweetheart, you'd better not write to the Daddy after 1 July. Won't be around to get it.

Love,
Vic (Big)

21 June 45
#21, Rasthaus am Cheim See

Hello, Sweetheart,

Came down yesterday to spend a day of leisure here. Had a fairly nice time dancing last night. Dance broke up at 0200, then went to bed. Had a nice room assigned to me. Been up since 0800 and plan on going on a sightseeing trip and then off to Berchtesgaden* for a picnic.

Boy, you should see this rasthaus. It is something out of a storybook. Has a staff of 163 people (skeleton crew) to run the place. They even turn down the beds and lay out your pajamas for you.

I'm waiting on the gang to start in on the sightseeing trip, so I thought I'd drop you my daily letter. Been pretty good about writing my Mommy, haven't I? Have written some of those letters during some pretty hot periods too. Didn't think I could do it.

I love you.

Vic (Big)

*Adolph Hitler had maintained a retreat in this resort town in southeast Germany.

22 June 45
#22, Simbach, Germany

Good morning, Mommy,

Back in the saddle again after my day's recreation. For our sightseeing trip yesterday we took in the Alpine Scenic Road through the Alps to Berchtesgaden. Honey, I could write volumes on the beauty of Bavaria, but they wouldn't tell you half of it. I have never seen or even imagined that any place could be as beautiful as this part of Germany. You have to see it to believe it.

They tell me that there are other places that are even more beautiful. One Italian-American nurse in our crowd says that Italy and Switzerland are far superior in beauty. I don't believe it — can't see how it is possible.

I'm running out of words, so you'll just have to wait until I can describe it to you personally.

I love you.

Vic (Big)

23 June 45
#23, Simbach, Germany

Good morning, Mommy,

Here it is another day — packing day for us. We are really busy now, packing all our stuff, getting ready to leave. Tomorrow we move out of our billets into the field. We bivouac by the railroad tracks so we can get onto the train without a lot of marching. Necessary 'cause we have turned in our vehicles.

I dread the thought of the train ride. Trains we have aren't worth a damn. All the good trains are on the other side of the river in Austria, but because of blown bridges, we can't get them over here. Everyone rides in a boxcar. Very uncomfortable. It will take us about 3 1/2 days to make a 500 mile trip.

We can take anything as long as we are headed in the right direction.

I love you.

Vic (Big)

24 June 45
#24, Simbach, Germany

Good morning, Mommy,

Sunday again. Probably will be the last one spent in Deutschland. Although we've had a fairly pleasant stay here, this no fraternization rule has taken the real fun out of it. No fraternization not only means you can't fool around with the frauleins (although that in itself isn't so hot), but it also means absolutely no talking with Germans, no shopping in German stores, no going into beer parlors, etc. We might as well be on a desert island.

The troops in France, Belgium, Czechoslovakia, Italy, etc., are all having a hell of a good time, but the gang here are about fed up. Hope we get in on some of the fun in France.

I love you.

Vic (Big)

25 June 45
#25, Simbach, Germany

Hello, Mommy,

Had to break up my old routine of writing you your letter first thing in the morning on account of having spent last night in the field. The mommy's and the Daddee's pictures are packed away in my footlocker.

If everything goes according to schedule, we should leave here tomorrow. We go via Munich, Augsburg, Stuttgart, Nancy, then to a port I am not permitted to give you the name of.

Everyone is really excited about being able to go home, and we all are looking forward to that 30 day leave.

I love you.

Vic (Big)

26 June 45
#26, Simbach, Germany

Good morning, Mommy,

Well, here it is at last — the day we start on our long trek home. We've broken up camp and are all ready to mount our train, which is scheduled to leave at 1230.

We've had a fairly nice time camping in the open for a couple of days, but after the luxurious life we've grown accustomed to, it was a bit on the rough side.

I haven't received any mail from you for over a week because all our mail had been directed to Rheims. Am looking forward to receiving a huge batch there.

I'm beginning to count the days 'till I see my Mommy again.

I love you very much.

Vic (Big)

CHAPTER V

LAST DAYS IN EUROPE: PREPARING FOR HOME

"A DAY HASN'T GONE BY WHEN I HAVEN'T THOUGHT OF YOU
AND OF BEING REUNITED WITH YOU."

The 500-mile train trip from Simbach, Germany to the redeployment Camp Atlanta in Mailly, France took three and a half grueling days. The upbeat mood of the soldiers on their way back to fraternization country must have been tempered by the grim view from the train of the German cities devastated by Allied bombs. Passing through Stuttgart, my father observed, "We've really been getting a good look at what the Air Corps did to German cities. They didn't miss very much." Once the train crossed into France, the Americans were gratified by the welcome they received from the citizens of such places as Avricourt, who recognized them from four months before, when they had passed through on their way to the battlefront.

Once he had arrived at Camp Atlanta on June 29, my father's thoughts turned to one important piece of unfinished business: tracking down his brother Underwood, who had been listed as "missing in action" since August 1944, when he was captured by Germans in Normandy. My father's repeated attempts to arrange a flight to Brest failed — bad weather grounded him for several days, and when the weather finally cleared, time had run out. No doubt my father had hoped that he would find his brother alive and well, as he had found his childhood friend, Bill Ghiz, in Braunau. Instead, he ended up having to cancel the trip to Brest. The knowledge of Undy's fate would remain a mystery for several more months.

One other sobering reality had to be confronted: in his July 5 letter he emphatically told my mother that he intended to remain in the Army "until the war is over," which meant in Japan also. At this time, the men of the 13th Armored Division fully expected to return to America, enjoy a 30-day leave, and then be redeployed to Asia. The atomic bomb attacks on Hiroshima and Nagasaki in August 1945 hastened an end to the war in Asia, and spared the division from further combat. Nevertheless, in July 1945, my father and his battalion knew only that probably they would soon be ordered to Asia.

On a happier note, my father wrote that once he was settled back in Normandy, he planned to revisit Beaunay, where his European sojourn had begun. In his July 12 letter, he reported, "Our friends at the château went all out on a big lun-

cheon for us," after which he and other American soldiers toured the surrounding villages and were given an enthusiastic heroes' welcome. The only sad part, he said, was "when they asked for someone who had been killed."

In the final days before his departure from France, my father's mood became quite romantic and sentimental, no doubt in anticipation of his reunion with my mother. Writing from Fauville,

A photo of my father taken in Germany in June 1945.

France on July 13, he recalled the 1938 Worcester Trade School Ball, which both he and my mother attended, each of them with a different date. He remembered that his date was quite annoyed with him because he was paying so much attention to my mother. "Heck, I didn't want to hurt her feelings," he recalled. "I just couldn't help it. Besides, couldn't she tell I was in love with you? Everyone else could."

The 13th Armored Division left Le Havre on July 14, fittingly the French Day of Independence. Just before his departure, my father wrote one last letter from Europe. His purpose was clear: to assure my mother that during their long separation he had thought of her and my brother every day. As if to put to rest any concerns she might have about changes he had undergone, he wrote that he was "the same as the day I left you. The only change is that [I love] you more."

27 June 45
#27, Stuttgart, Germany at 0800

Good morning, Mommy,

Here it is the Daddy's birthday, and is it pouring cats and dogs. Imagine, I'm 31 now. Really getting old now, although if you'd watched me playing ball night before last, you'd never have thought so.

I've been rereading the so very nice birthday card you sent me. You sure pick some humdingers. Just about everyone back home remembered my birthday and sent me greetings.

Right now our train is moving through Stuttgart on our way home. We've really been getting a good look at what the Air Corps did to German cities. They didn't miss very much. Railroads are jammed with DP's and PW's on their way home. Everyone, it seems, belongs someplace else.

I love you.

Vic (Big)

28 June 45
#28, Between Avricourt and Lunéville, France at 0700

Good morning, Sweetheart,

Here we are back in fraternization country. It may not be as pretty as Deutschland, but it sure is a welcome sight to these eyes 'cause it means that we are that much nearer home.

We started our operations against the Germans by jumping off from this same town of Avricourt 4 months ago. When we pulled into the station, many of the people recognized us and gave us quite a welcome.

We stop at Nancy for our breakfast — all I have to say is God help any French girls who may be hanging around the railroad station. That lovestruck gang of mine is going to be a problem.

I love you.

Vic (Big)

29 June 45
#29, Mailly, France

Good morning, Mommy,

Here we are at last at the redeployment camp finishing packing, getting rid of stuff, and getting ready to go home. We are the first outfit to go through here. After all that talk about fraternization, we find ourselves isolated in a camp 30 miles from the nearest village. Ow!

Found letters dated 11, 12, 14, 18, and 19, as well as the phonograph records, awaiting me. Thanks a million, bud.

You don't have to have another examination by a doc if you don't think it necessary. It's just that I want so badly to get some company for my little man.

Mommy, you are getting my letters a bit twisted. I've been sick but once, and that with the grippe, which was brought on by exhaustion and the lack of sleep for 12 days. Never felt better.

I love you.

Vic (Big)

30 June 45
#30, Mailly, France

Hello, Sweetheart,

Been pretty busy today trying to arrange a plane flight to Brest to check up on Undy. Believe it or not, Brest is 550 miles away and over some of the worst roads in the country. Gen. Auger has been really swell and has gone to a great deal of trouble trying to arrange the plane flight for me. Please don't say anything to my folks about my trip to Brest yet. Let me handle that end.

Say, young lady, you're getting to be pretty bold. Since when did you start talking about midnight snacks, etc.? I've read back letters of yours, and I'm a bit frightened.

I don't know when we leave here, but it should be soon. Can't tell you where we are to land — don't know anyway. However, will end up at Ft. Devens. How about a ride home, bud?

Love,
Vic (Big)

1 July 45
#1, Paris, France

Hello, Mommy,

I was extremely lucky and was able to get a plane to fly me to Brest. However, we had to stop here at the Paris airport to get some flight information. At the present moment we are waiting for the weather to clear. Damn, it's been raining for a week now. As soon as we get the go sign, we take off.

You know, Sweetheart, we weren't very lucky in our selection of a boat to bring us to Europe, but I believe we are going to hit the jackpot on our return trip. Rumor has it that we return on one of the super lines*. Not permitted to say which. Read the newspapers — they usually have more information than we anyway.

I love you.

Vic (Big)

*The ship that brought the 46th Tank Battalion home was the Holland-America Line's *Noordam*, a definite improvement over the *Sea Quail* that brought them to Europe.

2 July 45
#2, Paris (damn) France

Good morning, Sweetheart,

Damn! We're still grounded. What a rotten break 'cause if we don't get out of here soon, I must return. I sure would hate to do that without checking up on Undy.

Mommy, confidentially and on your word of honor: From the tone of the folks' letters I am worried that they may be planning some kind of a reception or such. Please, if you love me even just a little bit, don't let them go through with it. I'd write and tell them except that I don't really know that they are, and I don't want to hurt their feelings. However, knowing them and how they tend to magnify anything I may have done, I believe I have good cause to worry. Please don't let them embarrass me.

Love,
Vic (Big)

3 July 45
#3, Paris, France

Good morning, Sweetheart,

Weather is impossible so I am returning to Camp Atlanta, where I hope there is still time to make other arrangements to get to Brest.

Mommy, I hope that you have been reading the papers about not meeting returning boats from Europe. You see, honey, you aren't allowed on the dock, nor are we free until we are processed through whatever post we arrive in. Takes a day. We then have to move in groups to Assembly areas. Mine is Ft. Devens. That takes another day. Then we are free.

DON'T TRY TO MEET THE BOAT. I'll call you as soon as we dock. I love you.

Vic (Big)

4 July 45
#4, Mailly, France

Hello Sweetheart,

Just got back from Rheims. Flew from Paris to here and then to Rheims in an attempt to get a larger plane to fly me to Brest. No luck. All planes are tied up in the move of the 2nd Armored Division to Berlin. Looks like I won't be able to get to Brest after all, as we are leaving this area this Sunday for the port. If the port happens to be Brest, I'll be able to take care of it; otherwise no luck*.

---

*After the war, when the details of Underwood's death were revealed, the Abdelnour family had his body brought back to the United States. He was buried in Los Angeles, where the family planned to relocate. Many years later, the city of Worcester honored Underwood by naming Abdelnour Square, located at the intersection of Commonwealth Avenue and Hamilton Street, after him.

Honey, I've written you about not meeting the boat. Please don't try as you can't get to see me anyway. Ft. Devens is the first place I can contact you. I'll call you when I get to whatever port it is we arrive at. So stay home like a good girl. I should be home with you within a week of Ah-Goo's birthday.

I love you.

Vic (Big)

5 July 45
#5, Mailly, France

Hello, Sweetheart,

Writing this letter while I am taking a bath. Received your letter of 23 June. Very surprised to receive it, as all our mail has been stopped at the New York post office.

Look, Toots, here is how I get my 92 points, and they are only figured to May 12.

Length of Service (1 pt. each month)	56
Overseas credit (1 pt. each month)	4
Dependent children (12 each)	12
Battle stars 2 (5 each)	10
Decorations 2 (5 each)	10

I have the highest score in the battalion.

Staying in means until the war is over. Has everyone forgotten the dirty Japs? You should know me better than to think I'd include points I anticipate.

I love you anyway.

Vic (Big)

6 July 45
#6, Mailly, France

Hello, Sweetheart,

Another lazy day of lolling around in the sun. First clear day we've had in two weeks.

By the time you get this letter, Ah-Goo should be two years old. Please wish him a happy birthday for me, and tell him I'll be home real soon afterwards.

The boys are all beginning to get restless now. Been here too long. We've been ready to leave for the past five days, but I guess the ships aren't ready for us yet. Anyhow, latest dope is we leave here Monday for an area nearer the port. Don't know how long we'll be there, but it shouldn't be more than two days.

Counting the minutes until I see my little family again. Where will we stay for the month that the Daddy has off? My folks' house will be a bit crowded with Vicki there.

I love you.

Vic (Big)

7 July 45
#7Mailly, France

Good morning, Mommy,

As you probably know by now, we are scheduled to complete our training at Camp Cooke, California. If the Mommy would like to go to that windy, crowded country with the Daddy, how about asking Vicki to rent us a place in Santa Maria. I suppose Vicki is going back soon. If not, forget it. I'll have my brother Eddie take care of it for us. Thought I'd get the jump on everyone else on renting a house. Ought to be rented for about the 23rd of August on. We were supposed to go to Cooke in February of '41 with the 5th Armored, but I got moved to the 8th. Remember?

They have a prevailing wind of 30 mph. Foggy till 10 in the morning. Rough, eh, kid? Did Ah-Goo have a nice birthday?

I love you.

Vic (Big)

9 July 45
#9, Mailly, France

Hello, Sweetheart,

It is now just 1800, and we are getting our train ready for the move. We leave at 2224 for our port, and then after a short stay there, home, you, little Victor, and all the folks. Can hardly wait to see you all.

Went to a dance at Rheims last night, and was in the process of crossing the dance floor on the way to getting some Cokes, when a nurse detached herself from her partner, ran over, and threw her arms around my neck. After I got over the embarrassment and got a good look, I found Olga Botzchea, my old nurse galfriend who took care of me when I had the operation on my foot at Beale. I was the first person that she knew from home that she had run into in 18 months overseas.

I love you.

Vic

10 July 45
#10, Fauville, France

Hello, Sweetheart,

Just pulled into our new and temporary camp home. It is located between Rouen and Le Havre and is not very far from Beaunay. I think I'll run
up tomorrow and see all our friends there.

Don't know yet what port we leave from or when, but it should not be
very long now. If this letter reaches you before Ah-Goo's birthday, please
give him an extra big kiss and a nice present from me. Tell him his Daddy
will be home real soon too.

Right now I'm trying to get my boys bedded down before it gets dark.
Doesn't get dark until 10:30 pm here. Gets light again about 4 am. That's
because we are further north than you are in Worcester.

Nothing much more now except to say that I'm counting the seconds till
I see you.

Love,
Vic (Big)

11 July 45
#11, Fauville, France

Hello, Mommy,

Got up pretty late this morning. Real tired after packing that doggoned
French train for 22 hours. We've got a million things to do in our packing because of a thousand and one forms we have to fill out for the cus-
toms.

Doesn't look as though I'll be able to get off to go to Beaunay. Weather
is miserable. Looking forward to more pleasant weather at home.

Everyone is really excited about going home. Honestly, you'd think we hadn't been home in 10 years. At that our division is pretty lucky [at this point the ink is barely visible, then changes abruptly to very dark ink]. Out of ink — new pen.

I hope you've got my summer uniforms all cleaned up for me. Don't put that soldier suit on Ah-Goo to greet me with. Anything else.

I love you.

Vic (Big)

≈)(≈

12 July 45
#12, Fauville, France

Hello, Sweetheart,

It is now 1700 and the Daddy (Big) has just gotten back from Beaunay. While there I visited all my friends and, what with taking a drink at each friend's house, I'm a bit on the wobbly side. Our friends at the château went all out on a big luncheon for us. Really swell.

We toured the villages after lunch, and boy did the people turn out to wave and say hello to us. They really are proud of our battalion in this part of France. Really made us feel swell. The only sad part of the thing was when they asked for someone who had been killed. Even that didn't dampen our good spirits, though.

Counting the minutes.

I love thee.

Vic (Big)

13 July 45
#13, Fauville, France

Good morning, Sweetheart,

In one of my previous letters, I stated that it did not get dark till 10:30pm. I was wrong. Last night it wasn't quite dark at midnight. Days sure are long.

Don't know why but my mind has been running back to the old Trade School Ball of 1938. Remember, I thought you'd invite me but you didn't. I still laugh (although I shouldn't) when I think of Frankie getting sick on you what with the full moon and all. Remember how I got that corsage for you and how I sneaked in every other dance with you, even though you have always been a lousy dancer? I still scream every time I think of how sore the girl I was with got because she thought (and rightly) that I was paying too much attention to you. Heck, I didn't want to hurt her feelings. I just couldn't help it. Besides, couldn't she tell I was in love with you? Everyone else could.

I love you.

Vic (Big)

14 July 45
#14, Le Havre, France

Good morning, Sweetheart,

This is a particularly hard letter to write 'cause it should be the end of the long European story you have been receiving from me in driblets. All that I can say is that in the time I have been away, I have learned to love you and my little shadow more and more with each passing day. A day hasn't gone by when I haven't thought of you and of being reunited with you. It is hard to believe that at last this hope is now being realized.

I can assure you that the Daddy looks the same and is the same as the day he left you. The only change is that he loves you more. Please fix things at home so that we three can be our own little family as much to ourselves as possible.

I love you very much.

Vic (Big)

CHAPTER VI

THE VOYAGE HOME

"CAN HARDLY WAIT TO HOLD THE MOMMY IN MY ARMS."

On the 10-day voyage home, my father wrote eight more letters. In the first one, dated July 15, a new and somewhat surprising word appeared in my father's vocabulary: "nervous." A few days later, on July 18, he confided that "I haven't gotten over my nervousness about going home yet," and he concluded his July 21 letter, "Still nervous." The next day he finally confronted the reasons for his anxiety, which were two-fold. First, knowing that his parents "[must] feel so bad about Undy" understandably caused emotional stress in the son who had survived the war.

In addition, he believed that the fact that "people [in the neighborhood] embarrass me so much when I am home also has a good deal to do with [my nervousness]." Although my father delighted in the admiration he received from Worcester family members and friends, he was ill at ease with their tendency to exaggerate the achievements of the homeboy who had become a hero. The local papers had diligently followed the events of the war, and had devoted considerable space to the 46th Tank Battalion and its commander, sometimes confusing the facts a bit, as my father pointed out in his May 16 and June 11 letters.

At first the sea was extremely rough, causing seasickness among most of the men aboard ship. Even my father, who had bragged that he had felt fine on the voyage to Europe, admitted that "I haven't gotten sick yet, but I know plenty of times when I have felt better." For those who felt up to it, recreation consisted of movies and the organization of a musical band. The band in particular won praise from my father, who loved to dance and always drew attention when he took to the dance floor.

As the ship crossed time zones, my father reset his watch, mentally getting in sync with life back in the USA. One can easily imagine the exuberance of the American soldiers as they passed Nantucket Lighthouse on July 22 and glimpsed America for the first time in six months. As my father recounted, "All the boys from around New England threatened to jump off the ship and swim to shore."

The last document in the correspondence is a Western Union telegram, sent from Camp Kilmer, New Jersey, and dated July 23, 1945. It speaks for itself.

15 July 45
At Sea

Dearest Mommy:

We set sail yesterday morning at 0600. That would be Friday night at 2400 your time, as there is six hours difference in time.

All day we've been able to sight the south coast of England on our starboard side. The sea is as smooth as glass. Weather beautiful. Ship we are on is far more comfortable than the ships we came over on, although the men are a bit more crowded.

Somehow or other I'm a bit nervous about going home. Don't know why. Just feel that way. Hope I get over it by the end of the trip. Trip should take ten days at the most. I should be home with you by the 25th. I had had hopes of getting home for Victor's birthday, but that's out.

Love,

Vic (Big)

16 July 45
At Sea

Hello Sweetheart,

Weather still beautiful. Hope it holds out. Can't see the English coast any longer. Sure a lonesome feeling being out on the ocean. This ship is a really nice one. Far superior to the usual troop ship. We were really lucky to get it. Food is finest I've eaten anywhere.

On board with us are the 67th and the 124th, and that is all. Again we are lucky. We were the first ship in our division to set sail, and that two days ahead of schedule. We understand that some units of the division do not leave until the 20th. Thank God we are on our way.

You can't imagine how happy the men are. Europe was miserable for them. No good times of any sort. I'm sure glad I could speak the language. I had some fun.

I love you.

Vic (Big)

⁓⁓

17 July 45
At Sea

Hello Mommy,

Weather has taken a sudden turn for the worse. We are bucking strong head winds, which are cutting down our speed considerably. Sea is really rough. Men are sick all over the ship. Poor Feldman — he's the worst sailor on board — has gone to bed. He won't get up until the storm is over.

Up to now we've seen quite a few ships, but today just one went by us headed for Europe.

Food on the ship is really something to rave about, but who the heck feels like eating now? For entertainment we've had movies twice. In addition, we've organized a band, which is something to listen to. It's as good as most dance bands at home.

I love you.

Vic (Big)

⁓⁓

18 July 45
At Sea

Dearest Mommy,

The storm got worse steadily. By supper half the men on board were in misery. Father Crawford lost his meal right at supper table, which caused about four more people to lose theirs. Can't get Feldman, Weaver, or O'Malley out of bed. Sheffey and I are still holding out.

Later at 1700

After a day and a half of pounding, the sea has quieted down again. We're cleaning up the ship again so it's livable. Have a movie and a dance music concert scheduled for this evening.

Saw a ship headed for Europe and misery at 1600. Really lonesome feeling.

I haven't gotten over my nervousness about going home yet.

I love you.

Vic (Big)

19 July 45
At Sea

Hello, Sweetheart,

Been at sea 5 days now and we are well past the halfway mark. We've had 25 hours in each of our days so far 'cause we set the clocks back one hour every night. Now there is but one hour difference in time.

We had a really nice concert last night. About 2100 a plane flew overhead on its way to Newfoundland. Was a welcome sight 'cause you don't see much out here. Right now it is 1400 and we haven't had any company as yet today.

The sea began getting rough again a bit after midnight and is becoming rather heavy now. Feldman just went to bed. Anyone who goes to sea merely for pleasure ought to have his head examined. I haven't gotten sick yet, but I know plenty of times when I have felt better.

Tomorrow is Victor's birthday. Hope you have a nice party for him.

I love you.

Vic (Big)

20 July 45
At Sea

Hello, Mommy,

Weather has taken a sudden turn for the better. Perfect day, but for the first time getting hot. It is now almost midnight, at which time we make our last time adjustment — same time as you from now on.

The Daddy is awfully tired and pretty tight right now. I figured out the time difference between here and Yuba City*, and at 18 minutes after noon I started celebrating my Daddee's birthday. I've just stopped, so you can see I've been celebrating about 11 hours and am I tired and whoozy. I've never drunk so much liquor in one day in my life.

Half the officers in the battalion were drunk by 9 o'clock, at which time I quit counting them. The outsiders on the ship thought we were crazy to be celebrating as we did, but they tolerated us.

The gang really like the shadow. I really missed not being with him on his birthday, but I held up my end of the celebration. How did you all do?

Mommy, just a little while ago, I was on deck watching the three quarter moon. It made me awfully homesick for you. Last full moon I spent the whole night looking at the moon and thinking of you and hoping I'd be with you for the next. Looks like my wish will come through 'cause I certainly should be home by the 25th (full moon).

I love you.

Vic (Big)

*the city in California where my brother was born

21 July 45
At Sea

Hello Sweetheart,

It is now 1630 and I just came from seeing the movie "Going My Way." We saw it together last fall at Camp Bowie. Got up a bit late after sleeping like a dead man. Boy, I was really tired after that celebration we had yesterday.

The sea is fairly calm today, but the sky is cloudy. It was beautiful up till about 1000. We are approximately 600 miles from New York now. We should arrive first thing Monday morning.

Dope has it that we go to Pier 16 at Staten Island. We then go to Camp Shank or Kilmer, where the men will be issued their cotton clothing and segregated into Reception Center groups, and we hope then shipped to our Reception Center (Devens) by nightfall Monday. We then spend one day at Devens getting paid, getting leave orders, etc.

When this is done, off we go to home. Can't begin to tell you how anxious I am to get home. Still nervous.

I love you.

Vic (Big)

22 July 45
Off Nantucket Lighthouse

Hello, Mommy,

It is now 1800 same time as you have. We are about two hours off the Nantucket Lightship and about 14 hours or 225 miles out of New York. We are scheduled to arrive at 0800. Should be off the ship by noon.

It's been awfully foggy all day with several rain squalls. Everyone is starting to pack. All the boys, including your Daddy, are rather excited.

Now 2300. Passed Nantucket Lightship at 1945. The blasts of their foghorn sounded really welcome. All the boys from around New England threatened to jump off the ship and swim to shore. Good idea but a bit on the wet side.

Why should I feel so nervous about going home? I guess because my folks feel so bad about Undy, and secondly 'cause I never did like our neighborhood. The fact that people embarrass me so much when I am home also has a good deal to do with it.

Can hardly wait to hold the Mommy in my arms. Is she still a cold number? I love you.

Vic (Big)

The last "letter":

WESTERN UNION

1201

(20)

A. N. WILLIAMS
PRESIDENT

This is a full-rate Telegram or Cablegram unless its deferred character is indicated by a suitable symbol above or preceding the address.

DL = Day Letter
NL = Night Letter
LC = Deferred Cable
NLT = Cable Night Letter
Ship Radiogram

The filing time shown in the date line on telegrams and day letters is STANDARD TIME at point of origin. Time of receipt is STANDARD TIME at point of destination

NA343 10=CAMPKILMER NJER 23 616P

MRS VICTOR DELNORE CARE ABDELMASEH= 1945 JUL 23 PM 7 29

=34 ALMONT AVE WCSTR=

=ARRIVED CAMP KILMER SHOULD BE HOME WEDNESDAY NIGHT PHONE
TOMORROW=

=VICTOR.

THE COMPANY WILL APPRECIATE SUGGESTIONS FROM ITS PATRONS CONCERNING ITS SERVICE

AFTERWORD

T he dropping of the atomic bombs on Hiroshima and Nagasaki hastened the end of the war in Asia and changed the Army's plans to
send the 13th Armored Division to attack Tokyo Bay. But, as it turned
out, the U.S. Army did have plans for my father that involved the Far East.
Although he did not go as a combat soldier, a year after the war ended he
was sent to Japan in a very different capacity. On September 23, 1946, Lt.
Col. Delnore was named Commander of the Nagasaki Prefecture Military
Government Team. As Military Governor of an area about equal to the state
of Massachusetts in size and population, he was responsible for overseeing
the initial stages of reconstruction and recovery of one of the seven major
political subdivisions of that defeated country. My father's highly acclaimed
achievements are recounted in detail in Lane Earns' essay "Victor's Jus-
tice," which appeared in the Summer 1995 volume of *Crossroads*, a journal
of Nagasaki history and culture.

During the first weeks in Japan, my father received from his parents a
letter containing news of the death of his brother Undy, who by this time had
been missing in action for over two years. From his post in Nagasaki, in a
letter to his parents dated October 15, 1946, my father wrote: "Just received
your letter telling me about the confirmation of the Mayor of Brest's story
about Undy. I am with you in your grief and hope that now that the story has
been confirmed...your grief will be short-lived...." He went on to describe
having recently attended a Buddhist ceremony commemorating the war dead,
during which he was very moved by the grief of the Japanese people, whose
faces "looked no different than the faces of the people at church back home;

the war widows and the war mothers looked just as bereaved as any of our womenfolk." My father recounted that during that Buddhist ceremony, he prayed "for the eternal peace and rest of the soul of my brother Undy. Honestly, I was deeply moved. Whether it was the strangeness of the ceremony, the numerous mourning womenfolk, or the boxes of the ashes of the 10,000 unclaimed and unidentified victims of the atom bomb that were piled all around the altar, I'll never know. All I do know is that I prayed for his soul as I have never prayed before. And this all before I received your letter." It seems clear that my father's profound empathy with the bereaved Japanese survivors in some way prepared him to accept the sad news of his brother's death.

In 1947, my mother and brother joined my father in Nagasaki, and a year later "company for Ah-Goo" arrived in the person of a baby sister, me. The following year, the Delnores returned to the United States for a series of domestic assignments at Ft. Monroe, Virginia; Ft. Leavenworth, Kansas; Quantico Marine Base, Virginia (where a third child, Cathy, was born in 1951); and Camp Lejeune, North Carolina.

In 1954, the Army sent my father back to Europe, this time to the Netherlands, to serve with the Military Assistance Advisory Group in administering

The military governor of Nagasaki and his wife look approvingly at Delnore Road, named in their honor.

May 1949: The Delnore family bids farewell to Nagasaki and begins the long journey back to the USA.

military aspects of the Mutual Defense Assistance Pact. The whole family accompanied him, settling in The Hague, where, a year later, he was promoted to full Colonel. During our three-year stay in Holland, we traveled every summer, and it was on one of these family vacations, while we were motoring through Germany, that my father pointed out to us the place near Manfort where he had been wounded in 1945.

The next tour of duty took the family 6,000 miles from Europe, to southern California, where my father served as senior Army member on the staff of the commander of the Pacific Amphibious Forces, headquartered at the Naval Amphibious Base in Coronado, California. This very pleasant experience for the whole family was followed by the one post-war hardship duty that my father was assigned. In the spring of 1961, he was named deputy chief of the U.S. Military Training Mission in Saudi Arabia, and he began a year-long assignment at the military base in Dahran.

When he returned from Saudi Arabia in 1962, it was to accept his last Army assignment. The family moved to Ft. Meade, Maryland, where my father served as commander of the Maryland-District of Columbia Sector of the XXI U.S. Army Corps. When the U.S. Army Reserves were reorganized in 1968, he became the first commander of the newly created U.S. Army

Advisory Group. While stationed in Maryland, my father pursued a lifelong dream to get a college education, and he earned both a bachelor's and a master's degree in history from the University of Maryland.

My father retired from active duty in 1969, and in 1970 he and my mother moved back to Massachusetts to fulfill another lifelong dream: they bought their first house. At the same time, the recent Army retiree embarked on a new career as a teacher at Middlesex Community College, near Boston, where he was twice named Teacher of the Year.

After a long Army career that took him and his family around the world, once my parents retired they realized that they didn't just want to be *near* their hometown of Worcester; they wanted to be *in* it. So in 1976, they moved one last time, to the Worcester suburb of Boylston. With great enthusiasm, my parents renewed friendships with childhood friends and relatives who had never left Worcester. My father accepted a teaching position at Worcester's Assumption College, and also began an active life as a volunteer. Over the years he contributed many thousands of hours, doing everything from answering the phones at the local Veterans Center to helping GIs at Ft. Devens fill out their tax returns. In addition, he became an active member of the Boylston Historical

The Delnore family, 1990, at my father and mother's 50th Anniversary party. Left to right: Patricia; Victor, Jr.; Catherine; Victor, Sr.; Cathy.

Society and of his boyhood Melkite Catholic parish, Our Lady of Perpetual Help. And every year he looked forward to attending reunions of the surviving members of the 46th Tank Battalion, sometimes accompanied by my mother. Although he was afflicted with Parkinson's disease, he did not let his illness prevent him from remaining active until the very end of his life.

But the end did come. In April of 1998, my father fell on the concrete basement steps at home and suffered a severe brain injury. He was rushed to the University of Massachusetts Medical Center, unable to move or speak. For much of his life, my father had struggled against tremendous obstacles — poverty, lack of education, ethnic discrimination, war, and debilitating illness. He had won all of those battles, but this battle he could not win. In a nursing home in West Boylston, Massachusetts, he died early one Sunday morning in late May, six weeks after his accident and just two days before my mother's birthday.

WHERE AND WHEN

MY FATHER'S ITINERARY

JAN. 16-JULY 23, 1945

January 16:	SS *Quail* departs New York Harbor
January 28:	ship docks in Southampton, England
January 29:	ship docks at Le Havre, France; disembarks
Most of February:	quartered with Wermaire family at their château in Beaunay, northwest of Paris
February 1:	visits Rouen, France
February 24-28:	visits Belgium (Liège) and Luxembourg
Approx. March 1:	visits Paris
Early March:	back with outfit in Beaunay
March 14 :	46th Tank Battalion ordered to Germany
April 15:	wounded in combat in Manfort, Germany; earns Purple Heart and Bronze Star

Approx. April 16:	Task Force Delnore reaches Schonenberg (near Zweibrucken)
April 17:	captures enemy troops, including two German generals in Mudlinghoven; earns Silver Star
April 29:	participates in liberation of POW camp in Worth, Germany
Early May:	participates in liberation of POW camp in Braunau, Austria (Hitler's birthplace); finds Bill Ghiz
May 8:	war in Europe officially over
May 21:	visits Salzburg, Austria; Berchtesgaden, Germany
June 5:	outfit moves from Braunau to Simbach, Germany (across Inn River)
June 20:	visits Chiem See, Germany
June 21:	visits Berchtesgaden
June 26-28:	returns to France (Simbach-Munich-Augsburg-Stuttgart-Nancy)
June 29-30:	46th Tank Battalion stationed at redeployment Camp Atlanta near Mailly, France
July 1:	goes to Paris (trying to get to Brest to check on brother Undy)
July 4:	travels from Paris to Rheims (still trying to get to Brest)

July 5-9:	returns to Mailly; has to cancel trip to Brest (bad weather prevents flying)
July 10:	stationed at temporary camp near Beaunay
July 12:	takes a day trip to Beaunay; reunion with Wermaire family
July 14:	sets sail from Le Havre on the Holland-America Line's Noordam
July 22:	sights Nantucket Lighthouse off Cape Cod, Mass.
July 23:	46th Tank Batallion arrives at Staten Island, then Camp Kilmer, NJ, then Fort Devens, Mass.

FAMILY PHOTOS

Victor Abdelnour, the young scholar (circa 1922)

Mrs. Nozly Abdelnour stands proudly with her son at Niagra Falls, New York (1940)

Army-Navy rivalry: my father "fighting" with his brother-in-law, Signalman 1st class Pete Abdelmaseh at Camp Beale, California (1942). The two men corresponded during World War II while Pete was stationed in the South Pacific, but none of those letters have survived.

My father and his newborn son, Victor, Jr., at Camp Beale, California (1943)

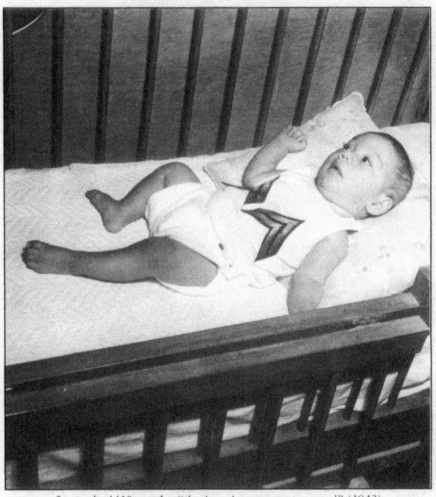

2-month old Victor, Jr., "the Army's youngest corporal" (1943)

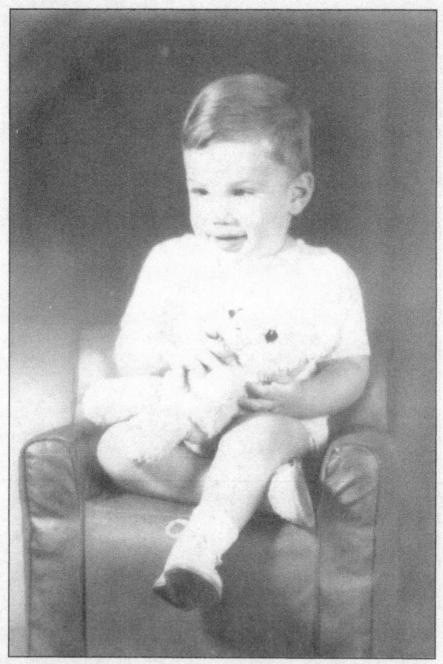

Victor, Jr. (a.k.a. "Ah-Goo," "my shadow," "Daddee") in Brownwood, Texas, in November 1944, shortly before my father's departure for Europe

My parents, wearing Japanese costumes, in Nagasaki (1947)

Catherine (kneeling) and Victor, Jr., posing with other Americans stationed in Nagasaki (1947)

Patricia's christening at Oura Cathedral in Nagasaki: the family poses with Archbishop Paul Yamaguchi, who officiated (Dec. 19, 1948)

Mother and daughter: Catherine and Patricia (1948)

A very different mother/daughter photo: Catherine and Patricia in Japanese costumes in the garden of the Nagasaki residence (March 1949)

Catherine, Victor, Jr., and Patricia visiting one of Nagasaki's sacred shrines (April 1949)

Catherine and the three children standing in front of our apartment building in The Hague, Netherlands, where my father served from 1954-57 with the Military Assistance Advisory Group

"Mini" family reunion at my parents' home in Boylston, Massachusetts, in April 1998. Seated, from left to right, are daughter Patricia, Victor, son-in-law Tim Collins, and granddaughter Christina Collins. Standing, from left to right, are Catherine, son-in-law James Magee, granddaughter Rebecca Collins, and daughter Catherine Delnore Collins. This photo was taken just days before my father's fatal accident.

A DISTINGUISHED CAREER

First Lieutenant Victor Delnore shortly before he married Catherine (1940)

The Delnore home in Nagasaki: official residence of the Military Governor

Lt. Col. Delnore with the staff of the Nagasaki Military Government Team (circa 1947)

Lt. Col. Delnore with members of the Japanese press (circa 1948)

Helen Keller on a visit to Nagasaki as the guest of Military Governor Lt. Col. Delnore, on October 16, 1948: From left to right are Miss Keller; her companion, Polly Thompson; my father; and an unidentified woman.

Official photograph of Col. Victor Delnore taken shortly after he reported for duty as senior Army member on the staff of the commander of the Pacific Amphibious Forces. This assignment took the family to Coronado, California, from 1957-61.

Civilian and military dignitaries attend a luncheon at Andrews Air Force Base (1964). Left to right are my father, MD-DC Sector Commander, XXI USA Corps; Maj. Gen. Herbert Brand, CG, 310th Logistical Command; Judge Ralph Powers, 7th Judicial Circuit Court of Maryland; Maj. Gen. Van Bond, CG, XXI USA Corps; Mr. Carlos Dixon, President, Chamber of Commerce, Prince Georges County; and Brig. Gen. Lowell Bradford, Deputy CG, 310th Logistical Command.

Gen. Charles D'Orsa, Deputy CG Reserve Forces at Ft. Meade, Maryland, congratulates my father upon presenting him with the Legion of Merit at his retirement ceremony (September 1969).

My father attending an award ceremony to honor volunteers at the Memorial Veterans Hospital in Bedford Massachusetts (April 26, 1992). Presenting him with a silver cup in appreciation of his volunteer work is Jeffrey Honeycutt, Chief of Voluntary Services at the hospital.

My father at a reunion of the 13th Armored Division (undated photo). Pictured with him are fellow Black Cat veterans Fulton Gale (left), Commander of the 45th Tank Battalion; and Charles Yon (center), Commander of the 24th Tank Battalion.

Printed in the USA
CPSIA information can be obtained
at www.ICGtesting.com
LVHW011128090824
787694LV00003B/326